Safe Conduct

BORIS PASTERNAK

SAFE CONDUCT

an autobiography and other writings

A NEW DIRECTIONS PAPERBOOK

CONTENTS

INTRODUCTION
by Babette Deutsch

The biography of a poet is found in what happens to those who read him. Pasternak says this in speaking of the effect upon him of another poet, Rainer Maria Rilke. It is in key with their shared way of seeing the world as process, of seeing the artist as one who transforms, by the power of his emotion, the physical events his senses perceive into that which the spirit greets.

This view was fostered by the circumstances of Pasternak's personal history. His father, Leonid Pasternak, was a celebrated painter, his mother, Rosa Koffman-Pasternak, a great musician. The Moscow in which their eldest son, Boris, was born, in 1890, surrounded him with more than the usual marvels, invited him to more than the usual adventures of childhood. Music was literally in the air he breathed, especially the ecstatic music of the family friend, Scriabin. Among the portraits that occupied his father—who years later would paint such diverse transformers of the world as Lenin and Einstein—were those of Leo Tolstoy and Rilke. The boy's encounters with these two, however brief or tangential, were significant. As the adolescent Yeats had been a naturalist, so the child Boris was a passionate botanist. This too, of course, contributed indirectly to his poetry. Much of that poetry took the form of prose, but never adopted its pedestrian gait.

A perfectionist, the young Pasternak, because he lacked absolute pitch, abandoned music for law. An intellectual gourmand, he abandoned law for philosophy, Moscow for Marburg. Headed by the ardent neo-Kantian, Hermann Cohen, the Marburg school fed the young man's hunger for the discipline of science, for a generously inclusive idealism, for socially oriented ethics. The one element of Cohen's thinking that he could not accept, though he was himself a Jew and his father's work did not ignore Jewish themes, was the old philosopher's attachment to their common heritage. A trip to Italy taught him "the tangible unity of our culture," re-emphasizing his sense of the vital continuum of all art.

Then came the war. "Boys of my age," he says in his autobiography, "had been thirteen in 1905 and were nearly twenty-two before the war. Both their critical ages coincided with the two red dates in their country's history." Because, having broken a leg in his boyhood, he could not go to the front, he served the war effort in a factory in the Urals.

Before he left Moscow the young poet found himself on the fringe of other battles. The self-styled Futurists had declared war on the past with an impudence equalled only by their energy. Experimenting with rhyme and metrics, syntax and vocabulary, they scorned alike the academic dodoes and their own contemporaries at home and abroad, even their Italian progenitors. The most gifted of their leaders, Vladimir Mayakovsky, won from Pasternak, who was a few years his senior, a love just this side of idolatry. It was a devotion able to leap the gulf that was to separate a poet frankly apolitical from the man who became the laureate of the Communist regime. Mayakovsky shot himself in 1930. Pasternak, though at one time accused of belonging to the "internal emigration," lives to bear witness to the power that has always protected the eager and the doomed, that even at the outbreak of the first world war, "behind the trees along all the boulevards . . . stood on guard, a power terribly tried and experienced, a power that followed them with wise eyes. Art stood behind the trees, an art which discriminates so wonderfully in us that we are always at a loss to know from what non-historical worlds it has brought its skill to see history in silhouette." He has borne witness to this power in his lyrics, his stories, his translations from such poets as Verlaine, Goethe, Shelley, Shakespeare, in the frankness of his speech before the Board of the Union of Soviet Writers in 1936, most recently in his big novel, *Dr. Zhivago*. He bore witness in paying tribute to the genius of Mayakovsky, whom at the height of his prestige Pasternak confessedly could not understand, and in acknowledging, with mingled pain and admiration, that "his strangeness was the strangeness of our times of which half is as yet to be fulfilled." When he writes of this poet it is as if Mayakovsky were for him a symbol of the violent disruptions, the catastrophes and the births that Russia has endured in the past half century, yes, half century and more, for the February and November revolutions were partially shaped by the abortive revolution of 1905, which furnished material for a quasi-epic by Pasternak. "I returned to Moscow soon after the February revolution," he says. And in the next sentence: "Mayakovsky came down from Petrograd and stayed in the Stoleshnikov mews. In the morning I went to see him in his rooms." Presumably the two young men spoke of the political upheaval. It is certain that they talked about the future of Futurism, which

Pasternak wanted his friend to send to the devil publicly; it is certain that they read and discussed a new poem.

Pasternak's brief autobiography is dedicated to a poet of a totally different temper, Rainer Maria Rilke. That he is able to embrace the work of both is an expression of more than a brave catholicity of taste. It belongs to his view of culture as a living mosaic, of art as infinitely precious because it is perpetually presenting a fresh image of humanity, conceived with a passion like physical passion and endowed with a newness that "inwardly resembles a new promise." He says something of the sort in *Dr. Zhivago*. This novel includes a sheaf of lyrics purporting to be by the physician and poet whose name gives the book its title. It is hard to believe, at first, that they were actually written by his creator. The poems to which Pasternak had accustomed his readers are each a cluster of laminate, proliferous images, transforming and thus re-creating reality. The metrics may be traditional, but the rhymes, as I have tried to indicate in my versions, are oblique and apocopated. If those early lyrics suggest kinship with other work, it is with that of Hopkins or Dylan Thomas, rather than that of Mayakovsky or of Rilke. The latter, in the spring of 1926, was writing to Leonid Pasternak of "the young fame of your son Boris," saying that the last thing he had tried to read in Russian "were poems of his, very *beautiful* ones . . ." The lyrics by "Dr. Zhivago" are also beautiful, but in a fashion totally unlike that of Pasternak's previous pieces. These are simple in syntax and, even when symbolic, relatively modest in imagery; at least one is so direct and subdued that it recalls poems by such old masters as Tu Fu and Po Chü-I.

Pasternak possesses the gift, essential to durable

writing, of particularizing even seemingly trivial events in such a way as to enhance them, so that they take on universality, while drenched with the here and now. His conviction of the large integrity, the powerful radiance of art — painting, music, poetry — is confirmed for the reader by the recognitions that he is continually inviting. When he speaks of the history of culture, of the relation between the known, which "makes its appearance as legend, folded into the rudiments of tradition," and "the unknown, new each time" which "is the actual moment of the stream of culture," one is reminded not only of Eliot's insights but of the epilogue to Lu Chi's fourth century poem on the art of letters, the utility of which, he says, "extends over a thousand miles and nothing can stop its course; . . . penetrates a million years, the ferry from one to the other. Looking one way, it hands down the laws to the ages to come; looking the other way, it examines the symbols made by the men of old . . . and daily it is new." When Pasternak confesses his youthful love for "that instinct with the help of which we like salangane swallows build the world — an enormous nest, put together from earth and sky, life and death, and two times, the ready to hand and the defaulting," a nest sustained by the strength of imaginative energy, he is kindled by a fervor like that which illuminates Wallace Stevens' notes in prose and poetry "toward a supreme fiction." And when Pasternak adds apologetically, "But I was young," going on to assert the importance of "the experience of real biography," one is reminded of Stevens' insistence that "The real is only the base. But it is the base." The significance of the real is expressed metaphorically in a poem by the hero of Pasternak's novel. Ostensibly about March in the country, it points to the pungent dung-heap as the source of the glowing, burbling activity in farmyard, cowbarn, and stable. Throughout his work, and notably in his recent novel, there are pages that astonish and delight as would an encounter with any of the poets mentioned above, as also with such others as Pushkin, Joyce, Valéry, Demetrios Capetanekis.

It is not the grandeur of his themes that gives his performance scope and depth. Like lesser lyricists, he writes about nature, about love: a raindrop clinging to two flowers at once, the quality of the moment before a thunderstorm, the first glimpse of mighty mountains, a kiss, a parting. An event as usual as a girl's crossing the threshold of puberty furnishes him with matter for a story. If, as rarely, he writes a poem with political implications, it is to assert a truism that needs constantly to be reaffirmed: that the vitality and the virtue of poetry, as of every art, lies in the poet's ability to realize his own experience, large or little, in his independence of dictatorship, from the left and from the right, in his gift for linking the past with the future by work that is as old as sunrise, and as new. Pasternak's pages offer refreshment because of the simplicity of his approach — a simplicity of heart, he has a subtle intelligence — and because the intensity of his feeling never disorients the completeness of his candor. His early work shows the vigor and sensitiveness of youth; the later shows a compassion bred of more intimate understanding of the human condition in all its sad ambiguity. It shows the strength that enables a man to endure this knowledge. His poetry and his prose belong to that incredible organism which grows out of our lives and on which they depend for survival, the organism to which he gives the name of art.

SAFE CONDUCT

Autobiography

PART ONE

I

AN EXPRESS TRAIN was leaving Kursk station on a hot summer morning in the year 1900. Just before the train started someone in a black Tyrolean cape appeared in the window. A tall woman was with him. Probably she would be his mother or his elder sister. The two of them and my father discussed a subject to which they were all warmly devoted, but the woman exchanged occasional words with my mother in Russian, while the stranger spoke German only. Although I knew the language thoroughly I had never heard it spoken as he spoke it. And for this reason, there on a platform thronged with people, between two bells, this stranger struck me as a silhouette in the midst of bodies, a fiction in the mass of reality.

On our journey, nearer Tula, the couple re-appeared, this time in our compartment. They talked about not being able to rely on the express stopping at Kozlovka-Zaseka, and they were not certain whether the guard would tell the engine-driver in time to pull up at the Tolstoys. From the talk following this, I concluded that they were on their way to Sophia Andreyevna, because she was going to Moscow for the symphony concerts, and she had been to see us not long ago—an endlessly important theme which was symbolised by the initials Count L. N. and played an obscure role in our family yet one discussed to saturation point, though without suggesting the personality of a man. It was seen too far back in childhood. His grey hair, afterwards renewed in my memory by the drawings of my father, Repin and others, had in my child's imagination long been assigned to another old man whom I saw more often and probably later—to Nikolai Nikolaevich Gay.

Then they said good-bye and returned to their own compartment. A little later the rushing embankment was suddenly held in check by the brakes. There was a glimpse of birch trees. The buffers snorted and knocked against one another along the whole stretch of railway track. With relief a cloud-piled sky tore itself from the whirlwind of singing sand. Skirting the grove, an empty carriage and pair, flinging itself forward as though dancing the *russkaya*, hopped up to meet the passengers who had just got down. The silence of a road-way which had nothing to do with us was yet disturbing momentarily, like a shot. It was not for us to stop here. They waved their handkerchiefs in farewell. We waved back. We could just see how the coachman with his long red sleeves helped them up, how he gave the lady a dust apron, and raised himself a little to adjust his belt and gather in the long tails of his coat. In a moment he would start. Meanwhile a bend caught us up, and the wayside halt, turning slowly like a page that has been read, vanished from sight. The face and the incident were forgotten, presumably forgotten forever.

II

Three years went by and it was winter out of doors. The street was foreshortened by at least a third with twilight and with furs. The cubes of carriages and lanterns sped along it silently. An end was put to the inheritance of conventions interrupted even before this more than once. They were washed away by the wave of a more powerful right to succession—that of personalities.

I shall not describe in detail what preceded this. How in a mode of feeling, reminiscent of Gumilov's "sixth sense," nature was revealed to a ten-year-old. How botany appeared as his first passion in response to the five-petalled persistence of the plant. How names, sought out according to the classified text, brought peace to eyes of flowers that seemed filled with scent, in their unquestioning rush towards Linnaeus, as if from nonentity to fame.

How in the spring of 1901 a troop of Dahomeyan Amazons was on show at the Zoological Gardens. How for me the first sensation of woman was bound up with the sensation of a naked band, of closed ranks of misery, a tropical parade to the sound of a drum. How I became a slave to forms, earlier than one should, because I saw in these women the form of slaves too soon. How in the summer of 1903 in Obelenski where the Scriabins lived next door to us, the ward of friends of ours who lived beyond the Prot, was nearly drowned. How the student who rushed to her aid met his death, and subsequently she herself went mad after several attempts at suicide from the same steep place. How later, when I broke my leg, in one evening ensuring my absence from two future wars, and was lying motionless in plaster of paris, the house of these friends over the river caught fire and the shrill village fire alarm, shaking feverishly, rang like mad. How, taut like a kite in the sky, the jagged conflagration beat upon the air, and suddenly, wrenching the splintering latticework away with the chimney, dived head over heels into the layer of purple grey smoke. How my father's hair turned grey at the sight of the circling glare which reared

15

in a cloud above the forest road from two miles off, as he galloped with the doctor that night from Maloyaroslavitz, and was filled with the conviction that this was the woman dear to him, being burnt with three children, and with a 100-lb. weight on the plaster of paris, which she could not possibly lift without running the risk of crippling the leg for life.

I shall not describe this, my reader will do that for me. He likes fables and horrors and looks upon history as upon a tale which is continued without end. It is impossible to tell whether he wishes the tale to have a reasonable conclusion. He likes those places best beyond which his walks have never extended. He is submerged in prefaces and introductions but life opens for me only in the place where he is inclined to balance accounts. Not to mention the fact that the inner parts of history are stamped on my understanding in the image of impending death, in life too, I lived wholly only on those occasions when the wearisome preparation of parts was over, and having dined off the finished dish, a complete feeling burst into freedom with the whole extent of space before it.

And so, it was winter out of doors, the street was foreshortened by at least a third with twilight, and the whole day was in a rush. Falling behind the street in the whirlwind of snowflakes the lanterns raced in their own whirlwind. On the way from school the name Scriabin, all in snow, tumbled from the concert bill on to my back. I brought it home with me on the lid of my school-satchel, water trickled from it on to the window sill. This adoration struck me more cruelly and no less fantastically than a fever. On seeing him, I would turn pale, only to flush deeply immediately afterwards for this very pallor. If he spoke to me my wits deserted me and amid the general laughter I would hear myself answering something that was

16

not to the point, but what exactly—I could never hear. I knew that he guessed everything but had not once come to my aid. This meant that he did not pity me, and this was just that unanswerable indivisible feeling for which I thirsted. This feeling alone, the more fiery it was, the more it protected me from the desolation which his incommunicable music inspired.

Before his departure for Italy he came to take his leave of us. He played—that one cannot describe—he had supper with us, he started philosophising, became ingenuous, joked. I kept feeling that he was inwardly very bored. They started saying good-bye. Good wishes re-echoed. Into the general heap of parting benedictions fell mine like a clot of blood. All this was said on the move and the exclamations crowding in doorways gradually descended to the hall. There everything was repeated with a resumed impetuosity and with the hook of his collar, which would not slip into the tightly sewn loop for a long time. The door banged, the key turned twice. Walking past the piano, which still spoke of his playing with the whole fretted lighting of the music-stand, my mother sat down to glance through the études he had left, and only the first sixteen bars of the prelude had fallen together, full of some surprised preparedness, not to be rewarded by anything on earth, when I rolled downstairs and without a coat or hat, ran along the dark Myasnitzkaya to make him come back or see him just once again.

This has been experienced by everyone. Tradition has appeared to us all, it has promised us all a face, and it has fulfilled its promise to us all in different ways. We have all become people according to the measure in which we have loved people and have had occasion for loving. Tradition, hiding behind the nickname of the medium in which one finds oneself, has never been satisfied with the compound image invented about it, but has always sent us some one of its most decisive exceptions. Why, then, has the majority passed away in the guise of a blurred generality, barely tolerable and bearable? It has preferred the faceless to faces, frightened by the sacrifices which tradition demands of childhood. To love selflessly and unconditionally, with a strength equal to the square root of distance is the task of our hearts while we are children.

III

Of course I did not catch him up, but very likely I did not even think of that. We met again after six years on his return from abroad. This date fell full upon my adolescent years. And everyone knows how boundless adolescence is. However many decades accrue to us afterwards, they are powerless to fill that hangar, into which they fly for memories, separately and in crowds, day and night, like learner aeroplanes for petrol. In other words, these years in our life form a part which excels the whole, and Faust who lived through them twice, lived through the absolutely unimaginable, which can be measured only by the mathematical paradox.

Scriabin arrived and the rehearsals for "Extase" began immediately. How I would like now to change this title which smells of a tightly wrapped soap carton, for one more suitable! The rehearsals took place in the mornings. The way there lay through melting gloom, along Furkasovsky and Kuznetsky which lay submerged in icy bread in kvass. Along the somnolent streets the hanging tongues of the belfries sank into the mist. In each a solitary bell clanged once. The rest remained in friendly silence together, with the full restraint of fasting metal. Nikitskaya Street beat egg in cognac at the end of Gazetnoy Street in the echoing abyss of the crossroads. Noisily the forged sledge-runners rode into the puddles and the flintstone tapped under the walking-sticks of the members of the orchestra.

The concert hall resembled a circus during the hours of the morning cleaning. The cages of the amphitheatre gaped empty. Slowly the stalls filled. Driven against its will in the sticks into the winter half, the music slapped its paw from there upon the wooden front of the organ. Suddenly the public would begin to appear in an even stream, as though the town were being cleared for the enemy. The music was let loose. Many-hued, breaking into infinite fragments, multiplying itself lightning flash on flash, it leapt the platform and was scattered there. It was tuned up, it raced with a feverish haste towards harmony and suddenly reaching the pitch of an unheard-of blending, broke off at the very height of its deep sounding whirlwind, dying away and straightening up along the footlights.

It was man's first settlement in the worlds, revealed by Wagner for fictive beings and mastodons. In one place a lyrical dwelling not fictitious arose, materially equal to the whole universe which had been ground down for its bricks. Above the fence of the symphony burned Van Gogh's sun. Its window-sills were covered with Chopin's dusty archives. The inmates did not poke their noses into this dust, but actualised the best testaments of their fore-fathers in all their arrangements.

I could not hear this music without tears. It was engraved on my memory before it lay on the zincographic plates of the first proofs. There was nothing unexpected in this. The hand which wrote it had been laid upon me six years back with no less weight.

What had all these years been but the succeeding transformation of the living imprint, given up to the will of

19

growth? It was not surprising that in this symphony I met an enviably fortunate contemporary. Its proximity could not fail to be reflected on people near it, on my occupations, on my whole way of life. And this is how it was reflected.

I loved music more than anything else, and I loved Scriabin more than anyone else in the world of music. I began to lisp in music not long before my first acquaintance with him. On his return I was the pupil of a composer even now alive and well. I had only to go through orchestration. All sorts of things were said, but the only important thing is that even if only antagonistic things had been said I could not imagine a life not lived in music.

But I did not possess absolute pitch. That is the name given to the gift of knowing the pitch of any sounded note. The lack of a talent which did not have any real connection with general musical sense but which my mother possessed entire, gave me no peace. If music had been my profession, as seemed the case to an outsider, I would not have been interested in this absolute pitch, I knew that outstanding contemporary composers did not possess it, and that it is thought Wagner and Tchaikovsky did not command it. But for me music was a cult, that is it was that ruinous point to which everything which was most superstitious and self-denying in me gathered, and because of this, each time that my will grew wings on an evening's inspiration, I hastened to humble it in the morning, reminding myself again of my so-called defect.

All the same I had several serious works. Now I was to show them to my idol. I set about making arrangements for a meeting, one so natural in view of the friendship of our respective homes, with a characteristic excess of effort. This step, one which would have seemed importunate to me in any circumstances, grew before my eyes into a kind of sacrilege in actual fact. And on the appointed day, making my way to Glazovsky, where Scriabin was living for the time being, I was taking him not so much my compositions but a love which had long outgrown expression and my apologies for my imagined lack of tact to which I admitted I had been led unwillingly. The crowded number 4 squeezed and jolted these emotions, bearing them mercilessly to the terrifyingly approaching goal along the brown Arbat which was being dragged to the Smolensky by shaggy and sweaty cows, horses and pedestrians, knee-deep in water.

IV

I appreciated then how well trained are our facial muscles. Unable to breathe properly from nervousness I mumbled something with a dry tongue and washed down my replies with frequent swallows of tea so as not to choke or make matters worse in some other way.

The skin began to creep along my jaw-bones and the protuberances of my forehead, I moved my eyebrows, nodded and smiled, and each time I touched the creases of this mimicry upon the bridge of my nose, creases ticklish and sticky like cobwebs, I discovered my handkerchief clutched convulsively in my hand and with it again and again I wiped the large beads of sweat from my brow. Behind my head, spring, bound by the curtains, rose smokily over the whole mews. In front, between my hosts who were trying with redoubled talkativeness to guide me out of my difficulties, the tea exhaled in the cups, the samovar hissed pierced by its arrow of steam, and the sun, misted with water and manure, circled upwards. The smoke of a stump of cigar, wavy like a tortoiseshell comb, pulled its way from the ashtray to the light, on reaching which it crawled repletely along it sideways as though it were a piece of felt. I don't know why, but this circling of blinded air, the steaming waffles, smoking sugar and silver burning like paper, heightened my nervousness unbearably. It subsided when going across to the salon I found myself at the piano.

I was still nervous when I played the first piece, when I came to the second I had almost recovered my control, during the third I surrendered myself to the pressure of the new and unforeseen. Accidentally my gaze fell on the listener.

Following the progress of the performance, first he raised his head, then his brows, finally all flushed, he got up himself and accompanying the variations of the melody with the elusive variations of his smile, glided towards me on its rhythmic perspective. He liked all this. I hastened to finish. Immediately he began assuring me that it was clumsy to speak of talent for music when something incomparably bigger was on hand and it was open to me to say my word in music. Referring to the phrases which had flashed by he sat down to the piano, to repeat one which had particularly attracted him. The harmony was complicated and I did not expect him to reproduce it exactly, but another unexpected thing happened, he repeated it in the wrong key, and the flaw which had tormented me all these years splashed from under his fingers as his own.

And again preferring the eloquence of fact to the instability of guesswork, I trembled and started thinking along two lines of thought. If he would admit to me: "Borya, why even I have not got it," then it would be all right, then, it would mean that I was not binding myself to music, but that music itself was my fate. But if in answer the conversation turned on Wagner, Tchaikovsky, on piano-tuners and so forth—but I was already approaching the nerve-racking subject, and interrupted in the middle of a word was already swallowing in reply. "Absolute pitch? After everything I have said to you? And what of Wagner? And Tchaikovsky? And hundreds of piano-tuners who have it?"

We were walking up and down the room. He would put his hand on my shoulder or take my arm. He talked of the harm of improvising, about when, why and how one should compose. For examples of simplicity to which one should always aspire, he instanced his own sonatas, notorious for their complexity. He took his examples of culpable complexity from the most banal literatures of the romances. The paradox of his comparisons did not worry me. I agreed that formlessness is more complex than form. That an unguarded volubility seems attainable because it is empty. That spoilt by the emptiness of trite patterns we take just that exceptional copiousness coming after long desuetude for the mannerisms of form. Imperceptibly he came to more definite advice. He questioned me about my education and, learning that I had chosen the faculty of law on account of its simplicity, advised me to change without delay to the philosophical section of the historico-philological, which I duly did on the following day. And while he talked I thought over what had happened. I did not break my arrangement with fate, but I remembered the bad issue of my guess. Did this incident dethrone my god? No, never—it lifted him from his former height to yet another. Why did he deny me that most straightforward reply for which I so longed? That was his secret. At some time when it would be already too late, he would bestow upon me this omitted confession. How had he allayed his own youthful doubts? That too was his secret and it was this which raised him to a new height. However, it was long dark in the room, the lamps were alight in the mews, it was time to know when to go.

I did not know as I took my leave how to thank him.

23

Something welled up in me. Something tore and sought for freedom. Something wept and something exulted.

The very first rush of cool street air told of houses and distances. Their uproar rose skywards, wafted off the cobblestones in the general harmony of a Moscow night. I remembered my parents impatiently preparing their questions. However I might make my statement it would bear no interpretation except the very happiest. And it was only at this point that submitting to the logic of the forthcoming recital I faced the fortunate events of the day as a fact. They did not belong to me in such a guise. As accomplished facts they became matters auguring a future outcome only for others. However much the news I was carrying my people might excite me, I did not feel calm at heart. But much more like happiness was my admission that just this sadness could not be poured into anyone's ears, and that like my future, it would be left there below, down in the street, there with my Moscow, mine in this hour as never before. I walked along the side streets and crossed the road more often than was necessary. Absolutely without my being conscious of it, the world which only the day before had seemed innate in me forever, was melting and breaking up inside me. I walked along gathering speed at every corner and I did not know that that night I was already breaking with music.

Greece distinguished excellently among ages. She understood how to meditate on childhood which is as sealed up and independent as an initial integrated kernel. How greatly she possessed this talent, can be seen in her myth of Ganymede and many others which are similar. The same convictions entered her interpretations of the demigod and the hero. In her opinion, some portion of risk and tragedy must be gathered sufficiently early in a handful which can be gazed upon and understood in a flash. Certain sections of the edifice and among these the principal arch of fatalism, must be laid once and for all from the very outset in the interests of its future proportions. And finally, death itself must be experienced, possibly in some memorable similitude.

And this is why the ancients with an art that was generalised, ever unexpected, enthralling as a fairy-tale, still knew nothing of Romanticism.

Brought up on a demand never afterwards made on anyone, on a superworld of deeds and problems, she was completely ignorant of the superworld as a personal effect. She was ensured against that because she prescribed for childhood the whole dose of the extraordinary, which is to be found in the world. And according to her ways, when man entered gigantic reality with gigantic steps, both his coming out and his surroundings were accounted ordinary.

v

One evening soon after as I was setting out for a meeting of the "Sirdards," a tipsy society of some half-score poets, musicians and artists, I remembered that I had promised Julian Anisimov, who used to read excellent translations of Dehmel to the company, that I would bring another German poet whom I preferred to all his contemporaries. And again, as had already happened more than once before, the collection of poems *Mir zur Feier* found itself in my hands at a very difficult time for me, and went off through the mire of rain and snow on the wooden Razgulyai, into the humid intertwining of days gone by, of heritage and of youthful promise, to be crazed by the rooks in the attic under the poplars and return home with a new friendship, that is with the sensation of another door in the town, where there were still few of them. But it is time I described how I came to have this collection of poems.

25

The thing is that six years before in that December twilight which I undertook to describe here twice, along with the noiseless street which was watched everywhere by mysterious snowflake wrinkles, I had been going on my knees too, helping my mother to tidy my father's book-shelves. The printed entrails wiped with a duster and dabbed over their four sides had already been replaced in neat rows in the disembowelled shelves, when suddenly from one particularly rollicking and disobedient stack fell a book in a faded grey binding. Absolutely by chance I did not squeeze it back and picking it off the floor, afterwards took it to my room. A long time went by and I grew to like this book, and soon another one too which came to join it and was inscribed to my father in the same hand-writing. But still more time went by before I came to find out that their author, Rainer Maria Rilke, must be that same German whom we once left behind us on our journey a long time ago, in summer on the whirling embankment of a forgotten forest halt. I ran to my father to check my surmise and he bore it out, wondering why that should so excite me.

I am not writing my autobiography. I turn to it when a stranger's so demands it. Together with its principal character I think that only heroes deserve a real biography, but that the history of a poet is not to be presented in such a form. One would have to collect such a biography from unessentials, which would bear witness to concessions for compassion and constraint. The poet gives his whole life such a voluntarily steep incline that it is impossible for it to exist in the vertical line of biography where we expect to meet it. It is not to be found under his own name and must be sought under those of others, in the biographical columns of his followers. The more self-contained the individuality from which the life derives, the more collective, without any figurative speaking, is its story. In a genius the domain of the subconscious does not submit to being measured. It is composed of all that is happening to his readers and which he does not know. I do not present my reminiscences to the memory of Rilke. On the contrary I myself received them as a present from him.

VI

Although my story has encouraged one to expect it, I did not ask what music is or what leads up to it. I did not do this: not only because I woke up one night when I was three and found the whole horizon bathed in its light for more than fifteen years ahead and, owing to this, had no occasion to experience the problematics of music; but also because it no longer bears on our theme. All the same, I cannot avoid the identical question in connection with art as a preference, with art as a whole, in other words, in connection with poetry. I shall not answer this question theoretically nor in a sufficiently general form, but a great deal of what I shall relate will be an answer which I can give for myself and for my poetry.

The sun was rising from behind the post office and slipping along the Kisel'noy was alighting on Neglinka. It had gilded our side and from dinnertime it was making its way into the dining-room and the kitchen. The flat was in a government building with rooms which had been altered from classrooms. I was studying at the university. I read Hegel and Kant. This was the time when at each meeting with my friends abysses would open up, and now one, now another would step forward with some newly revealed opinion.

Often we roused each other at dead of night. The one to be woken was ashamed of his sleep as if it were an accidentally discovered weakness. To the fright of the hapless

27

domestics, who without exception were accounted non-entities, we set off there and then for the Sokol'niki, to the crossing over the Yaroslav railway. I was friends with a young girl from a wealthy family. It was obvious to every-one that I was in love with her. She participated in these walks only in theory on the lips of the more unsleeping and adaptable of us. I was giving a few tuppeny-ha'penny lessons so as not to take money from my father. In sum-mer, after the departure of my people, I would remain entirely on my own. The illusion of independence reached such temperance in my food that hunger was joined to everything else and put the last touch to the turning of night into day in the uninhabited flat. Music, with which I was still only postponing a parting, was already becom-ing interwoven with literature. The depth and beauty of Biely and Blok could not but unfold before me. Their in-fluence united with forcefulness in an original way, which excelled simple ignorance. The fifteen-year-old restraint from the word, as a sacrifice on the altar of sound, doomed one to originality as any crippled limb may doom to acro-batics. Together with some of my friends I had connec-tions with "Musaguet." [1] From others I learned of the existence of Marburg. Cohen, Natorp and Plato took the place of Kant and Hegel.

I am purposely characterising the life I led during these years at random. I could enlarge these symptoms or change them for others. But those which have been cited are suffi-cient for my purpose. Having thrown them out as though for an estimate to indicate what my reality was at that time, I shall ask myself at this point where and through what agency at work in it poetry was born. I shall not have to ponder my answer long. This is the one feeling which memory has retained for me in all its freshness.

It was born from the conflicting currents of these trends,

from the difference in their flux, from the falling behind of the more tardy and from their accumulation behind, on the deep horizon of remembrance.

Love rushed on more impetuously than all else. Sometimes appearing at the head of nature it raced the sun. But as this stood out in relief but seldom, it can be said that that which had gilded one side of the house and had begun to bronze the other, that which washed weather away with weather and turned the heavy portals of the four seasons of the year, moved onwards with a constant supremacy which was nearly always contesting with love. And in the rear on the outskirts of various distances the remaining trends ambled along. I often heard the hiss of a depression which originated other than in myself. Overtaking me from behind it frightened and complained. It issued from a reft daily round and seemed either to threaten putting the brakes on reality, or to implore joining it to the living air, which meanwhile had had time to pass on far ahead. And it was in this gazing back that what is called inspiration consisted. The more turgid, uncreative portions of existence were realised with particular vividness, in view of the great distance of their ebb. Inanimate objects acted even more powerfully. These were the living models of still-life, a medium particularly endearing to artists. Piling up in the furthest reaches of the living universe and appearing in immobility, they gave a most complete understanding of its moving whole, like any boundary which strikes us as a contrast. Their position marked a frontier beyond which surprise and sympathy had nothing to do. There science worked in search of the atomic components of reality.

But as there was no second universe whence one could lift reality from the first, taking it roughly by the fore-lock,

[1] A literary society—*Translator's Note.*

it was necessary for the manipulations which it incited, to take its symbol, in the way algebra does, a symbol constricted by the same single planeness in regard to size. Still this symbol always seemed to me only a way out of the difficulty and not a goal in itself. I always saw the goal as the change-over of the symbol from cold axles to hot, in letting the outlived on to the track and into the chase after life. My conclusions were not very different from what I think now: I worked it out then as follows. We take people as our symbols so as to overcast them with weather, set them in their natural surroundings. And we take weather, or what is one and the same, nature—so that we may overcast it with our passion. We drag everyday things into prose for the sake of poetry. We entice prose into poetry for the sake of music. This, then, in the widest sense of the word, I called art, set by the clock of the living race which strikes with the generations.

This is why the sensation of a town never answered to the place in it where my life passed. A spiritual pressure always cast it back into the depth of the perspective described. There, clouds jostled, blowing about, and pushing through their crowd the converging smoke of innumerable fireplaces hung athwart the sky. There, ruined houses dipped their porches into the snow, line by line as though along the length of quays. There, the rotting unsightliness of the vegetation was fingered over by the quiet drunken plucking of a guitar, and, having sat long over the bottle and become thoroughly hard-boiled, flushed respectables with their swaying husbands met the breaking wave of nightly cab-men at the exit and seemed to issue from the laughing fever of the hot tub to the birchlike coolness of the anteroom at the baths. There, people poisoned and were burnt to death, flung vitriol at their rivals in love, rode out in satin to the altar and pawned furs at the pawnbrokers. There, surreptitiously the varnished smiles of a decrepit order of things leered at one another, and there, getting out their books in expectation of my hour's lesson, my nursling second formers settled down, painted bright as saffron with imbecility. And there too, the grey-green half-spat-over university boomed and subsided in a hundred auditoriums.

Sliding the glass of their spectacles over the glass of their pocket watches, the professors raised their heads to observe the galleries and the vaults of the ceilings. The heads of the students showed up against their coats and seemed to hang on long cords in exact pairs with the green lamp-shades.

During these visits to town where I found myself coming daily as though from another, my heart invariably beat the faster. If I had gone to a doctor he would have supposed I had malaria. But these attacks of chronic impatience did not lend themselves to treatment by quinine. This strange perspiration was brought out by the stubborn clumsiness of these worlds, by their native obviousness which was uncontrolled from within by anything in its own favour. They lived and moved as if they were posing. Uniting them into a kind of colony an imaginary antenna of epidemic predestinedness reared itself in their midst. The fever set in just at the raising of this imaginary rod. It was given birth by the currents which this mast sent to the opposite pole. Conversing with the distant mast of genius it called some new Balzac from those regions to its own hamlet. But one had only to move away a little from the fatal rod for an immediate tranquillity to descend.

So, for instance, I felt no fever at Savin's lectures because this professor was not true to type. He read with a real talent which increased as his theme grew under his hand. Time did not take offence at him. It did not tear

31

itself away from his assertion, did not leap into the ventilator or rush headlong for the doors. It did not blow the
smoke back up the chimney and bursting from the roof
seize the hook of the tram-coupling which vanished in the
snowstorm. No, entering heart and soul into the English
Middle Ages or the Robespierre Convention, it enticed us
after it, and along with us everything which we could
imagine as lively beyond the high university windows, end-
ing only at the cornice.

I remained in good health too, in one of the sets of
rooms in cheap furnished lodgings where with a number
of students I gave lessons to a group of adult pupils. No
one shone here. It was sufficient that not expecting a reward from any quarter the instructors and instructed
united in a common effort to move from the dead point to
which life was prepared to nail them. Like the lecturers,
among whom were some of those retained by the university, they were not typical of their callings. Petty clerks and
office workers, workmen, waiters and postmen they came
here so that they might eventually become something else.

I was not feverish in their active midst, and, in the rare
moments when I was at peace with myself, I often turned
into a neighbouring mews from there, into one of the back
wings of the Zlatoustinsky monastery where whole unions
of florists had their quarters. It was at this very place that
boys who hawked flowers on the Petrovka laid in their
stock of the full flora of the Riviera. Wholesale merchants
had them sent from Nice and one could buy these treas-
ures from them on the spot for a mere nothing. I was
especially drawn to them during the change-over in the
school year, when I had discovered one fine evening that
lessons had been carried on without electric light for a
long time, and the shining twilights of March were fre-
quenting the dirty rooms more and more, and later did not

even remain behind on the threshold of the lodging-house at the conclusion of our lessons. The street was not covered by the low kerchief of the winter night as usually happened, and seemed to rise from underground at the exit with some dry tale on her barely moving lips. Along the strapping pavement the spring breeze shuffled. As if covered by a little live skin the outlines of the mews shuddered in chill tremors grown cold in waiting for the first star, whose advent the insatiable sky postponed wearisomely, with the same leisureliness as the recital of a fairy-tale.

The odorous gallery was stocked to the ceiling with empty wicker baskets covered with foreign stamps under eloquent Italian postal markings. In response to the felted grunting of the door a cloud of thick steam rolled out as though to satisfy a need and for that alone one's expectations were aroused, because something unutterably exciting could already be anticipated from it. In the open space opposite the entrance, in the depths of the gradually sloping room the young hawkers crowded at the fortress window and on receiving the wares which had been duly checked pushed them into their baskets. In the same room at a broad table the sons of the proprietor were silently steaming open the parcels newly arrived from the customs house. Bent back in two like a book the orange lining revealed the fresh core of the wicker box. The thickly intertwining tangle of chill violets was taken out all of a piece like a blue layer of Malagas dried in the open air. They filled the room which resembled a porter's lodge, with such a madding fragrance that both the columns of early evening twilight and the shadows lying in layers on the floor seemed to be cut out of a damp dark-mauve turf.

But the real wonders were still awaiting me. Walking over to the far end of the yard the proprietor, unlocking one of the doors of the stone shed, lifted the cellar trap-door by its ring, and in that moment the story of Ali Baba and the Forty Thieves was re-enacted in all its blinding dazzlement. On the dry space under the floor flaming like suns gleamed four "lightning" lamps and vying with the lamps, there ran a riot in huge tubs which were sorted according to colours and types, hot stacks of peonies, of yellow marguerites, tulips and anemones. They breathed and hustled one another anxiously. Wafted up with unex-pected force a wave of lighter perfume washed off the dusty fragrance of mimosa, watery and threaded with oc-casional needles of anise. This was the scent of the narcissi bright as liquor diluted to whiteness. But even here the black cockades of the violets won in that storm of rivalry. Occult and half-crazed like pupils without the white of the eye they mesmerised with their aloofness. Their sweet never-coughed-through breath filled the wide rim of the trapdoor from the cellar's depths. They covered one's chest with a kind of wooded pleurisy. This scent reminded one of something and then slipped away, duping one's con-sciousness. It seemed that a conception about the earth which the spring months composed on the theme of this scent, encouraged them to return year by year, and that the sources of the Greek belief in Demeter were some-where very near at hand.

VII

At this time and for a long while to come I regarded my efforts at verse-making as an unfortunate weakness and did not expect any good to come of it. There was a man, S. P. Durylin, who gave me the support of his approval even then. This was explained by his unprecedented sensi-tiveness. I carefully hid these signs of a new adolescence

34

from the rest of my friends who had already seen me almost find my feet as a musician.

On the other hand I studied philosophy with wholehearted enthusiasm, presupposing in its nearness the beginnings of a future settling-down to the real business in hand. The round of subjects read in our group was as distant from the ideal as were the methods employed to instruct them. It was a peculiar mix-up of moribund metaphysic and cheerless enlightenment. Reconciling the two tendencies bereft them of the last remnants of meaning which might yet have remained to them had they been taken separately. The history of philosophy turned into a *belles-lettresistic* dogmatism, and psychology appeared as breezy triflings in brochure style.

The young assistant professors like Shpet, Samsonov and Kubitzki could not change this arrangement. However, the senior professors were not so much to blame for it either. They were tied down by the necessity of reading in a popular style down to the abecedarians who counted even in those times. Definitely not reaching the consciousness of the participators the campaign for the liquidation of the unlettered was begun just at this time. Students who had had some sort of preparation tried to work on their own, depending more and more on the model university library. Sympathies were divided among three names. The majority were enthusiastic for Bergson. The devotees of the Göttingen Husserlites found support in Shpet. The followers of the Marburg school were bereft of guidance and, left to themselves, sponged on the accidental ramifications of a personal tradition, still coming down from S. N. Trubetski.

The outstanding phenomenon of the circle was young Samarin. A direct descendant of the best Russian past and bound to it by different grades of family relationship with the history of the edifice itself along the corners of Nikitski, he would make an appearance about twice a semester at a meeting of some seminar or other, like the son who had received his inheritance and was returning to his parent's house at the hour of the general concourse for dinner. The reader of the paper would stop, waiting, till the lanky eccentric, abashed by the silence which he had inspired and was prolonging by his choice of a seat, would clamber over the creaking floor to the furthest bench of the boarded amphitheatre. But no sooner had the discussion of the paper begun, when all the clatter and squeaking which had just been dragged with such difficulty under the ceiling, returned below in a renewed and unrecognisable form. Attacking the lecturer's first reservation Samarin would pour out from there some impromptu from Hegel or Cohen, rolling it like a ball along the ribbed recesses of the huge cupboard-like warehouse. He would get nervous and swallow his words, and he spoke in an innately loud voice, keeping it on that even note which was always the same, his own from childhood to the grave, a voice which was ignorant of whispering and shouting and along with a round burr inseparable from it, always revealed his stock at once. Having lost sight of him in later years, I was involuntarily reminded of him when on re-reading Tolstoy I stumbled into him again in Nekhlyudov.

VIII

Although the summer coffee room on the Tverski Boulevard did not have a name of its own, everyone called it the *café grec*. It was not shut down for the winter and then its designation became a strange puzzle. One day without any previous arrangement, Loks, Samarin and I met accidentally in this bare pavilion. We were the sole guests not only that evening but perhaps for the whole season past. The weather had broken up for warmer days, spring was drawing on. No sooner had Samarin made his appearance and sat down with us than he began philosophising, and arming himself with a dry biscuit, he began breaking up the logical units of his narrative with it as with a choir-master's tuning-fork. A slice of Hegel's infinity stretched across the pavilion, composed of alternating theses and antitheses. Probably I had told him the theme I had chosen for my finals thesis and this led him to leap from Leibniz and the mathematical infinity to the dialectical. Suddenly he started speaking about Marburg. This was the first description of the town and not of the school which I had heard. Later I was convinced that it is impossible to speak of its antiquity and poetry other than like this, but at that time this enamoured description made to the clatter of the ventilator fan, was new to me. All of a sudden recollecting with a rush that he had not come there to drink coffee but only for a minute, he startled the proprietor, nodding in a corner behind his paper, and on learning that the telephone was out of order tumbled out of the starling-loft covered with ice, even more noisily than he had entered it. Soon we too rose to go. The weather had changed. The wind had risen and was beginning to scald with the February grain. It fell to the ground in regular skeins, in figures-of-eight. There was something of the sea in its violent loops. Thus layer on undulating layer they fold cables and nets. On our way Loks started off on his favourite theme of Stendhal several times, whilst I preserved a silence which the whirlwind favoured considerably. I could not forget what I had just heard, and I regretted the little town, which I was no more likely to see, as I thought, than my own ears.

That was in February and one morning in April my mother announced that she had saved from her earnings and economised from the household expenses two hundred roubles, which she was giving me with the advice that I should go abroad for a bit. It would be impossible to imagine my joy, nor the complete unexpectedness of the present, nor my undeservingness. It must have been necessary to endure a great deal of strumming on the piano for such a sum. But I did not have the strength to refuse. There was no need to choose a route. In those days European universities were constantly kept well informed of each other's doings. I began running round the information bureaux that same day and together with countless documents I brought a certain treasure from the Mokhovaya. This was a detailed description of courses to be read during the summer term of 1912, and printed in Marburg two weeks previously. Inspecting the prospectus pencil in hand, I would not part from it en route nor at the barred counters of official places. My agitation was catching from a mile off, and infecting secretaries and clerks, without knowing it, I was speeding up a procedure which was quite simple enough as it was.

Naturally my programme was a Spartan one: third class, and abroad if necessary fourth class in the slowest train, a room in some cottage near the town, bread, sausage and tea. My mother's self-sacrifice bound me to a tenfold avarice. On her money I ought to get to Italy as well. Besides I knew that a very considerable part would be swallowed by the entrance fee to the university and the fees for the separate seminars and courses. But even if I had had ten times the money I would not have departed from my list of expenses at that time. I don't know how I would have spent the remainder but nothing on earth would have made me change over to second class or incline me to leave my traces on the restaurant cloth. Indulgence with regard to my convenience and the need for comfort arose in me only in postwar times. It put such obstacles in the way of a world which did not allow any fineries or luxuries into my room, that my whole character could not but change temporarily.

IX

The snow was still melting with us, and in pieces the sky was sailing out into the water from the frozen crusts like a picture slipping from under the transfer paper, but in the length and breadth of Poland apple trees were in warm bloom, and it raced past from morning to night and from West to East, in summer sleeplessness, as some Romance portion of the Slavonic design.

Berlin seemed to me a city of young striplings who had received the day before presents of swords and helmets, pipes, real bicycles and suits, like grown-ups. I met them on first going out, they had not yet got used to the change and each one felt very important that he had received a plentiful share yesterday. In one of the finest streets Natorp's logic reader beckoned to me from a bookshop window and I went in to get it with the feeling that to-morrow I should see the author in person. During two days travelling I had already spent one sleepless night on German soil and now I had another before me.

Folding-beds in the third class are only made with us in Russia, abroad on a cheap journey one has to pay the penalty all night nodding four together on a deeply worn bench divided by armrests. Even though on this occasion both benches in the compartment were at my service I was far from sleeping. Only very rarely and at long intervals single passengers one after another, mostly students, entered and bowing silently vanished in the warm night obscurity. At each of their changes sleeping towns rolled beneath the platform roofs. The immemorial medieval age was disclosed to me for the first time. Its reality was fresh and frightening like every original. Clanging familiar names as on naked steel, the journey took them one by one from read descriptions, as from dusty scabbards, prepared by the historians.

In its flight up to them the train stretched out like a chain-mail wonder wrought from the ten-times-riveted carriage-frames. The small leather corridor connections dilated and expanded like a blacksmith's bellows. Pawed by the station lights, beer in clean beakers shone clear. Along the stone platforms empty luggage barrows disappeared smoothly into the distance on wide stonelike rollers. Under the arches of gigantic passenger-bridges sweated the torsos of flat-snouted locomotives. It looked as if they had been borne to such a height by the play of their low wheels which had unexpectedly died down in full action.

From all sides its six-hundred-year-old forefathers drew towards the desert-like concrete. Quartered by the slanting beams of the woodwork the walls varied their sleepy tale. On them crowded pages, knights, ladies and red-bearded cannibals, and the pattern of chequered beams in the woodwork was repeated like an ornament on the barred visors of the helmets, in the slits of the spherical sleeves and in the criss-cross cords of the waistbands. The houses came almost flush with the open carriage window. Towards the end thoroughly shaken up I lay oblivious of self on its wide rim, murmuring abrupt exclamations of a delight, now far from new. But it was still dark and the leaping paws of wild vines were only just darkening against the plaster. When the hurricane burst once more, smelling of coal, dew and roses, then suddenly drenched with a handful of flashes from the hands of the absorbedly racing night, I would lift the window quickly and begin thinking how impossible it was to foresee the events of the next

40

day. But I must somehow say something about the place to which I was going and why.

A creation of the genius, Cohen, prepared by his predecessor in the Chair, Frederick Albert Lange, famous to us for his *History of Materialism*, the Marburg school attracted me by its two characteristics. In the first place it was independent, it uprooted everything from its first rudiments and built on a clear space. It did not accept the lazy routine of all conceivable "isms," which always cling to their stock of omniscience at tenth hand, are always ignorant, and always for some reason or other afraid of a revision in the fresh air of age-old culture. Unsubjected to a terminological inertia the Marburg school turned to the primary origins, i.e., to the authentic signatures of thought, bequeathed by it to the history of knowledge. If current philosophy tells what this or that writer thinks, and current psychology, of how the average man thinks; if formal logic teaches how to think in a baker's so as to get the right change, then the Marburg school was interested in how science thinks in its twenty-five centuries of uninterrupted authorship, at the burning commencements and conclusions of the world's discoveries. In such a disposition, authorised, as it were, by history itself, philosophy was unrecognisably rejuvenated and made wise, transformed out of a problematic discipline into an immemorial discipline of problems, which is what it ought to be.

The second characteristic of the Marburg school derived directly from the first and consisted in its selective and exacting attitude to historical development. That repellent condescension to the past was foreign to the school, and it did not look down on it as on a poorhouse where a handful of old men in chlamyses and sandals or perukes and long jackets utter their lying and obscure lines, excusable for the wonders of the Corinthian order, the Gothic,

41

Baroque or some other architectural style. The homogeneity of the structure of science was as much the rule for the school as the anatomical identity of historical man. They knew history in its entirety at Marburg, and were never weary of dragging treasure after treasure from the archives of the Italian Renaissance, from French and Scottish Rationalism and other badly studied schools. At Marburg they gazed at history through both of Hegel's eyes, i.e., with brilliant universality, but at the same time within the exact boundaries of a judicious verisimilitude. So for instance, the school did not speak of the stages in the development of the "*Weltgeist,*" but, say, of the postal correspondence of the Bernoulli family, though it knew that every thought of however distant a time, surprised in its place and at its task, must be laid bare to our logical commentary. Otherwise it loses its immediate interest for us and submits to the guidance of the archeologist or the historian of costumes, characters, literature, social and political tendencies and so forth.

Neither of these traits of independence and historicism tell anything about how Cohen's system was upheld, but I did not mean, and would never undertake, to speak of its nature. Still, both explain its attractiveness. They show its originality, i.e., the vital place it occupies in a tradition vital to one section of contemporary knowledge.

As one of its small component parts I rushed to the centre of attraction. The train was crossing the Harz. In the smoky morning leaping from the wood, the thousand-year-old Goslar flashed by like a medieval coal-miner. Later Göttingen rushed past. The names of the towns grew louder and louder. The majority of these the train flung back in its way at full speed without stooping down to them. I found the name of these spinning tops on the map. Round some, ancient facts rose. These were attracted into their circling like stars meeting stars. Sometimes the horizon widened out as in *The Terrible Vengeance*, and smoking simultaneously in several orbits, the earth in the different little towns and castles began to undulate like the evening sky.

X

During the two years preceding my trip the word "Marburg" never left my lips. Mention of the town in chapters on the Reformation was made in every book on the subject for secondary schools. A booklet on Elizabeth of Hungary, buried there in the beginning of the thirteenth century, was even published for children as an "Intercessor." [2] Any biography of Giordano Bruno named Marburg among the towns in which he read on his fatal journey from London to his native land. And by the way, however improbable it may seem, I did not once in Moscow connect the identity existing between the Marburg of these recollections and the one for the sake of which I gnawed tables of derivatives and differentials, jumping from Maclaurin to Maxwell, who was definitely unapproachable for me. I had to snatch up my bag and pass the inn for knights and the old post-stage, for it to strike me for the first time.

I stood craning my neck and breathing hard. Above me towered a dizzy height on which in three tiers stood the stone *maquette* of the university, the town hall and the eight-hundred-year-old castle. After my tenth step I ceased to understand where I was. I remembered that I had forgotten my tie with the rest of the world in the railway carriage, and it was not to be recalled now any more than the hooks, the luggage-racks and the ashtrays. Above the clock-tower clouds stood festively. The place seemed

[2] Name of an edition—*Translator's Note.*

43

familiar to them. But they too explained nothing. It was obvious that as the guardians of this nest, they were not to be parted from it. A mid-day silence reigned. It communed with the silence of the plain stretched out below. They seemed to rise to the sum total of my bewilderment. The higher passed to the lower in a weary wave of lilac. Birds chirruped expectantly. I scarcely noticed the people. The motionless contours of the roofs were filled with curiosity —how would it all end?

The streets clung to the steeps like Gothic dwarfs. They were situated one below the other and their basements gazed over the attacks of their neighbours. Their narrow ways were filled with wonders of boxlike architecture. The floors which widened out upwards lay on protruding beams and, their roofs almost touching, they stretched out their hands towards each other over the road. They had no pavements. You could not walk freely in all of them.

Suddenly I realised, that a day must have preceded the five-year strollings of Lomonosov along these same bridges, when he first entered this town with a letter of introduction to Christian Wolff, a student of Leibniz, and still knew no one there. It is not enough to say the town had not changed. One had to realise that it might well have appeared just as unexpectedly small and medieval even for those days. And turning one's head, one could be jolted, repeating exactly one terribly distant bodily movement. As in the days of Lomonosov scattered at one's feet with the whole grey-blue swarm of its slate roofs, the town resembled a flock of doves enticed in a lively flight towards their cot at feeding time. I was in a flutter as I celebrated the second centenary of someone else's neck muscles. Coming to myself I noticed that the décor had become reality, and set off to find a cheap guest-house to which I had been directed by Samarin.

PART TWO

I

I TOOK a room on the outskirts of the town. The house stood in the last row along the Giessen road. In this place the chestnut trees with which the road was planted and which stood shoulder to shoulder on parade, turned towards the right in full file. Glancing back for the last time at the stern hill with its ancient little town the road disappeared beyond the wood.

My room had a small ramshackle balcony which overlooked the neighbouring kitchen-garden. A henhouse, made from a carriage taken off the rails of the old Marburg tramway, stood there.

An old woman, the wife of a clerk, let the room. She lived with her daughter on a meagre widow's pension. The mother and daughter were alike. As always happens with women smitten by Basedow's disease,[3] they intercepted my gaze which was directed thievishly at their collars. In these moments I imagined children's balloons, drawn together at the ends which look like ears and tightly tied. Perhaps they guessed this.

Out of their eyes from which one wanted to release a little air by laying the palm of one's hand on their throats the old Prussian Pietism gazed at the world.

And yet this type was not characteristic of this part of Germany. Another predominated here, the Middle-German, and the first suspicion of a South and West, of the

[3] A disorder of the thyroid gland—*Translator's Note.*

existence of Switzerland and France, crept even into Nature. It was very appropriate to finger the pages of French volumes of Leibniz and Descartes in the presence of her green leafy riddles growing in the window. Beyond the fields which came up to the ingenious poultry-pen, one caught a glimpse of the Ockershausen countryside. It was a long district of long barns, long wagons and massive Percherons. From there another road stretched along the horizon. As it entered the town it was called *Barfüsserstrasse*. In the Middle Ages the Franciscan monks had been called barefoot vagabonds.

Most likely winter came to this place each year along this particular road. Because gazing out that way from the balcony one could imagine a great deal that supported this notion. Hans Sachs. The Thirty Years' War. Somnolent and unexciting scenery of a catastrophe which is historic when it is measured in decades and not by hours. Winters, winters and winters, and then at the lapse of the century, like the yawn of a cannibal, the first stirring of new settlements under the wandering clouds, somewhere far away in the wild-grown Harz, with names such as *Elend, Sorge*, and others like these, black scorched ruins.

Behind the house at an angle, luring bushes and reflections beneath it, flowed the river Lahn. Beyond it stretched the railway embankment. In the evenings the dull snorting of the kitchen spirit-stove was violently interrupted by the repeated ringing of a mechanical bell to the sound of which the railway barrier dropped of its own accord. Then in the darkness by the level-crossing a uniformed man would rise up, quickly sprinkling it from a can in anticipation of the dust, and in that second the train rushed by, casting itself convulsively up, down and in every direction. Sheafs of its drumlike light got into the landlady's saucepans. And the milk always ran over and burnt.

46

Upon the oily waters of the Lahn another star subsided. In Ockershausen lowed the cattle which had just been driven in. Marburg shone in an operatic glare upon the hill. If the brothers Grimm could come here again, as they came a hundred years ago, to learn law from the famous jurist Savigny, they would leave here once more as collectors of fairy tales. Assuring myself that I had the key to the front door, I set off for the town.

The immemorial citizens were already asleep. I met only students. They all looked as though they were performing in Wagner's *Meistersinger*. The houses which even in daylight resembled a *décor*, pressed more closely together. There was nowhere for the hanging lanterns flung across the road from wall to wall to play. Their light fell with its full force upon the sounds below. It bathed the shuffle of disappearing footsteps, and the bursts of loud German speech with light as pure as fleurs-de-lys, as if even the electricity here knew the legend handed down about this place.

A long, long time ago, about half a thousand years before Lomonosov, when the first January ushered in a perfectly ordinary year, the 1230th one on earth, down from the Marburg castle along these slopes came a live historic personality, Elizabeth of Hungary.

This is all so far away that if imagination reaches back so far, at the point where it meets this scene a snowstorm rises of its own accord. It breaks out from extreme cold in obedience to the rule of the conquered unattainable. Night will set in there, the hills be clothed with forests, in the forests wild beasts will come. And human manners and customs will be encrusted with ice.

The future saint, canonised three years after her death, had a tyrant confessor, that is, a man without imagination. The sober practitioner saw that penances imposed on her at the confessional brought her into a state of exaltation. In search of penances which would be a real torture to her, he forbade her to help the sick and the poor. Here legend takes the place of history. It seems she had not the strength for this. It seems that to make this sin of disobedience innocent, a snowstorm screened her with its body on her way to the town below, turning the bread into flowers for the duration of her nightly crossings-over.

This is how nature is sometimes forced to depart from its laws, when a convinced fanatic insists too firmly on the fulfilment of his own. It does not matter that the voice of natural right is here invested in the form of a miracle. Such are the criteria of authenticity in a religious epoch.

As it neared the university the road, flying uphill, grew more and more twisted and narrow. One of the façades, baked in the cinders of ages like a potato, possessed a glass door. It opened into a corridor which led out on to one of the sheer northern slopes. There was a terrace there bathed in electric light and with small tables arranged on it. The terrace hung above the drop which had once caused the countess such disquiet. Ever since then the town which had arranged itself along the route of her nightly descents, had stopped short on the slope, wearing the very appearance it had assumed towards the middle of the sixteenth century. The precipice which had tormented her spiritual peace, the precipice which compelled her to disobey a rule, the precipice still moved by miracles as before, strode well in step with the times.

From it an evening dampness was wafted. On it iron thundered sleeplessly, and alternately flowing together and flowing apart, the sidings spluttered back and forth in the dark. Something noisy was constantly falling and being raised up. Till morning the watery rumble of the dam held the even note which it had taken on deafeningly from night-

48

fall. The piercing scream of the circular saw accompanied in thirds the bulls in the slaughter-house. Something was constantly bursting and glowing, steaming and pouring down. Something wriggled and was overcast with painted smoke.

The cafe was frequented chiefly by philosophers. Others had their own. G—v, L—ts and some Germans were sitting on the terrace, afterwards they all received Chairs either in their own universities or abroad. Among the Danes, Englishwomen, Japanese and all those who had come together from all corners of the world to hear Cohen, a familiar, burningly sing-song voice could already be distinguished. This was an advocate from Barcelona, a pupil of Stammler, a participator in the recent Spanish revolution, who had been completing his education here for the last two years, declaiming Verlaine to his friends.

I already knew many people here and was not shy of anyone. Already I had made two promises as I anxiously anticipated the days when I would be reading Leibniz with Hartmann and one of the sections of the *Critique of Practical Reason* with the head of the school. Already a mental image of the latter, long since guessed at, but appearing strangely inadequate at the first introduction, became my own property, that is, it gave rise in me to a spontaneous existence, which changed according to whether he plumbed the depths of my disinterested admiration, or floated on the surface, when with the delirious ambition of a novice I wondered whether I should ever be noticed by him and invited to one of his Sunday dinners. This last always raised a person in the esteem of the people there because it marked the beginning of a new philosophical career.

I had already verified in him, how a great inner world is dramatised when it has been presented with a great man.

49

I already knew how the crested old man in spectacles would lift his head and step back, as he held forth on the Greek conception of immortality and how he would wave his hand in the direction of the Marburg fire-station, in determining the shape of the Elysian Fields. I knew already how on some other occasion, having already stealthily arrived at pre-Kantian metaphysic, he would bill and coo and flirt with it, then suddenly clearing his throat, would give it a terrible reprimand with citations from Hume. How when he had finished coughing and made a long pause, he would say slowly, wearily and peaceably, "*Und nun, meine Herrn . . .*" And that would mean that the reprimand had been given to that century, the performance was over and one could move on to the subject of the course.

Meanwhile hardly anyone was left on the terrace. The electric light was being extinguished. It turned out that it was already morning. Glancing down over the rails, we were convinced that it was as if the nocturnal precipice had never existed. The panorama which had taken its place was oblivious of its nocturnal predecessor.

II

About this time the sisters V—— arrived in Marburg. They were from a wealthy family. In Moscow when still a senior schoolboy I was already friends with the elder of the two and used to give her lessons in goodness knows what at irregular intervals. More accurately, the family paid me for my chats with her on the most unpredictable topics.

But in the spring of 1908 our final terms and examinations at school coincided, and I undertook to coach the elder V—— concurrently with my own preparations for the exams.

The majority of my questions consisted of sections, which I had thoughtlessly omitted in their turn, when we were going through them in class. I had hardly enough nights to go through them now myself. But still at intervals, without bothering about times and more often than not at sunrise, I ran round to V—— for the lessons on subjects which always differed from my own because the order of our tests in different high schools was not in fact the same. This muddle complicated my position. I did not notice it. I had known about my feeling for V——, which was not a new one, since I was fourteen.

She was a beautiful and charming girl, perfectly brought up and spoiled from her very infancy by an old Frenchwoman who adored her. The latter understood better than I that the geometry which I brought her darling from outside at break of day was more Abelardian than Euclidian. And gleefully emphasising her sagacity she never left our lessons. Secretly I thanked her for her intervention. In her presence my feeling could remain inviolable. I did not judge it and was not judged by it. I was eighteen. In any case my general make-up and my upbringing would not have allowed me to give rein to my feelings.

It was at that time of year when paint is dissolved in little pots with boiling water, and out in the sunlight, left to their own devices, gardens warm themselves leisurely, loaded up with snow fallen from all sides. They are brimfull of quiet, clear water. And beyond their borders, on the other side of the fences, gardeners, rooks and belfries stand in ranks along the horizon and exchange loud remarks which can be heard over the whole town about two or three times a day. A wet woolly-grey sky rubs against the casement window, the sky full of a lingering night. Silent by the hour, silent, silent, and then suddenly it takes the round rumble of a cartwheel and rolls it into the room. It breaks off so unexpectedly that one would think this was a game of hide-and-seek and that the wagon had no other business but to slip from the road and in through the window. And that now it was safely "home." And the leisurely silence becomes more puzzling still, pouring in streams into the great hole hewn out by the sound.

I don't know why all this was imprinted on my mind in the form of a blackboard which has not been wiped clean of its chalk. O if we had been stopped then, if they had wiped the board till it shone moist and polished, and instead of expounding the theorem about the equal altitude of pyramids they had shown us in writing, emphatically, what was destined to befall us both. O how stupefied we would have been!

Whence comes this notion and why does it strike me here?

Because it was spring, which was roughly completing the eviction of the cold half-year and all around on earth lakes and puddles like mirrors which have not been hung, lay face upwards, and told of how the wildly capacious world was cleaned and its site ready for the new tenant. Because it was then possible for the first being who so wished, to embrace afresh and live through again all life which exists on earth. Because I loved V——.

Because even the perceptibility of the present is the future and a man's future is love.

III

But such a thing as the so-called noble attitude towards women also exists. I shall say a few words about it. There is that boundless circle of phenomena which evoke suicide in adolescence. There is also the circle of mistakes made by the infant imagination, childish perversions, youthful starvations, the endless circle of Kreutzer sonatas which get written to confute Kreutzer sonatas. I sojourned in this circle and lingered there shamefully long. What does all this mean then?

It tears one to shreds and nothing save harm ever came of it. And at the same time one can never get free of it. All who enter as people into history will always pass through it. Because these sonatas which make their appearance as the anteroom to the only complete moral freedom are not written by Tolstoy or Wedekind, but with their hands by Nature herself. And in their mutual inconsistency alone lies the fullness of Nature's design.

Basing matter on its resistances and separating fact from fancy with the dam known as love, she preoccupies herself with its durability as with the intactness of the world. Here comes the point of her obsession, of her morbid exaggerations. Here one can say truthfully that at every step she makes an elephant out of a fly.[4]

But no, I'm wrong, for nature makes elephants in real fact! They say that's her principal business. Or is that a mere phrase? And what about the history of aspects? Or the history of human names? And after all doesn't she prepare them all exactly here, in those places of live evolution which has been held back, at the dams, where her troubled imagination runs amok?

Could one not say then that in childhood we exaggerate and our imagination is disordered because at this time we are like flies and Nature makes us into elephants?

Holding to the philosophy that only the almost impossible is actual she has made sensation very much more difficult for everything alive. She has made it harder for the animal in one way, for the plant in another. The way in which she has made it harder for us speaks in her breathtaking opinion of man. She has made it harder for us not because we possess any automatic tricks but because we possess something which in her view endows us with absolute power. She had made it harder for us by the sense

[4] In Russian this phrase is equivalent to our "to make a mountain out of a molehill."—*Translator's Note.*

of our flylike triviality, which overcomes each of us the more strongly the further removed we are from the fly. This is expounded with genius by Andersen in his "Ugly Duckling."

All literature about sex, and even the very word "sex," smacks of an unbearable triviality, and in this lies its appointed significance. It is of use to Nature by virtue of just this repugnant quality because her whole contact with us is founded on our fear of triviality and anything which is not trite would not implement her means of controlling us.

Whatever the material our thought should provide in this connection the *fate* of this material is in her hands. And with the help of instinct which she has commandeered for us from her whole totality, Nature always disposes of this material so that all the pedagogic efforts directed towards the simplifying of Naturalism invariably overburden her, and that is how it *should* be.

It ought to be thus so that the feeling itself should have something to conquer. If not one panic then another. And it is of no consequence from what repugnance or nonsense the barrier is composed. The movement which gives rise to a beginning is the cleanest of all things known to the universe. And with this cleanness alone which has conquered so often through the ages it would be enough that by contrast everything else which is not it should smack of profound earthiness.

And there is art. It is concerned not with man but with the image of man. The image of man, as becomes apparent, is greater than man. It can come into being only in the act of transition and not in every one at that. It can only come into being in the transition from fly to elephant.

What does an honest man do when he speaks the truth only? Time passes in the telling of truth and in this time life passes onward. His truth lags behind and is deceptive. Should a man speak in this manner everywhere and always?

And in art he has to shut his mouth. In art the man is silent and the image speaks. And it becomes apparent that only the image can keep pace with the successes of Nature.

In Russian "to lie" has more the sense of "to exaggerate" than of "to deceive." In this sense does art lie. Its image embraces life but does not look for a spectator. Its truths defy description but are capable of unending development.

Art alone reiterating of love through the extent of the ages is not at the command of instinct to implement the means by which sensation is made harder. Taking a new spiritual development for its barrier a generation preserves a lyric truth rather than casts one off, so that from a very long distance one can imagine that apparently by virtue of this lyric truth humanity is gradually composed of generations.

All this is unusual. All this absorbingly difficult.

Taste teaches morality and power teaches taste.

IV

The sisters were spending the summer in Belgium. They heard from someone that I was in Marburg. At this point they were summoned to a family gathering in Berlin. On their journey there they wished to see me.

They stopped at the best hotel in the little town, in the most medieval part. The three days during which we were inseparable resembled my usual way of living as little as holidays resemble ordinary days. Telling them something or other continuously, intoxicated with their laughter and with the understanding expressions of chance passers-by, I would take them off somewhere. They were both seen with me at university lectures. And so came the day of their departure.

On the evening before, the waiter, as he set the table for supper, said to me: "*Das ist wohl ihr Henkersmahl, nicht wahr?* i.e., "Won't you eat a last meal; for to-morrow it'll be the gallows for you, eh?"

Next morning, on entering the hotel I bumped into the younger sister in the corridor. Glancing at me and realising that something was afoot she stepped back, without a greeting, and locked herself in her room. I went through to the elder girl and terribly nervous, said that it couldn't go on like this and I begged her to settle my fate. There was nothing new in this except my insistence. She rose from her chair backing away before the display of my anxiety which seemed to be pressing down on her. Suddenly by the wall she remembered that a means existed to put an end to all this once and for all and—she refused me. Soon a noise started up in the passage. They were dragging a trunk from the neighbouring room. Then they knocked at our door. Quickly I set myself to rights. It was time to go to the station. It was five minutes' walk.

There, the ability to say good-bye left me completely. I had just managed to grasp that I had only said good-bye to the younger sister and had not even begun with the elder, when the smoothly gliding express from Frankfurt loomed up at the platform. Almost in the same movement, quickly picking up its passengers, it started off again. I ran beside the train and at the end of the platform jumped at full speed on to the step of the carriage. The heavy door had not been slammed to. An excited conductor barred my way, at the same time grasping my shoulder so that abashed by his reasoning I would not take it into my head to risk my life. My travellers ran out into the corridor. They started pushing notes into the conductor's hand for my rescue and the purchase of a ticket. He took pity and I followed the sisters into the carriage. We were speeding towards Berlin. The fairy-tale holiday was continuing with

56

hardly an interruption, and was intensified tenfold by the frenzied motion of the train and by a blissful headache due to everything which I had just experienced.

I had jumped in while the train was moving simply to say good-bye, and now I forgot about it again and only remembered when it was too late. I had hardly recollected this when I found the day was gone, evening had set in, and pressing us towards the earth, the roof of the Berlin platform was rushing upon us and snorting. The sisters were to be met. It was undesirable that they should be seen with me in my present upset condition. They convinced me that we had said good-bye and that I had merely not noticed it. I vanished in the crowd which clustered together in the gaseous din of the station.

It was night and an evil drizzle descended. I had no business in Berlin whatsoever. The next train in the direction I wanted was leaving first thing in the morning. I could have waited for it at the station. But I found it impossible to remain among people. My face was twitching and my eyes constantly filled with tears. My thirst for a last finally ravaging farewell remained unquenched. It was like the longing for a huge cadenza, which would shatter an ailing music to its roots so that it would all suddenly be transported far away at the descent of the final chord. But I was denied this alleviation.

It was night and an evil drizzle descended. It was just as smoky on the asphalt in front of the station as on the platform where, like a ball in a string net, the glass dome hung inflated in its iron framework. The chink of street against street resembled carbon-dioxide eruptions. Everything was overcast by the quiet fermentation of the rain. On account of the unexpectedness of my situation I was in the clothes in which I had left the house, that is, without an overcoat, without luggage, without papers. I was shown out of lodging after lodging when they had taken one look at me, with polite protestations about their being full up. At last I found a place where my travelling light did not constitute an objection. These were lodgings which one would normally take only as a last resort. Finding myself alone in the room I sat sideways on a chair which stood by the window. There was a little table next to the chair. I dropped my head on the table.

Why do I describe my posture in such detail? Because I remained in it the whole night long. Occasionally as though at the touch of something I lifted my head and did something with the wall which drew away from me obliquely below its dark ceiling. I measured it as with a foot-rule from below with my unseeing intentness. Then my sobbing would start afresh. And again I would drop my head in my hands.

I have described the position of my body in such detail because this was its morning position on the bench of the flying train and was memorised for that reason. It was the posture of a person who had fallen away from something high which had long upheld him and long borne him onwards, until finally it let him fall and noisily speeding by above his head vanished forever behind a bend.

At last I got to my feet. I examined the room and flung open the window. The night had gone and the rain hung in a misty dust. It was impossible to say whether it was still raining or whether it had stopped. I had paid for the room in advance. There was not a soul in the hall. I left without a word to anyone.

v

It was only here that I suddenly saw something which had probably begun earlier, but had all the time been hidden by the proximity of what had happened and by the ugliness of the sight of a grown-up weeping.

I was surrounded by transformed objects. Something

never before experienced crept into the substance of reality. Morning recognised my face and seemed to have come to be with me and never to leave me.

The mist dissolved promising a hot day. Gradually the town began to move. Carts, bicycles, vans and trains began slithering in all directions. Above them like invisible plumes serpentined human plans and designs. They wreathed and moved with the compression of very close allegories which are understood without explanations. Birds, houses and dogs, trees and horses, tulips and people became shorter and more disconnected than when childhood had known them. The laconic freshness of life was revealed to me, it crossed the street, took me by the hand and led me along the pavement. Less than ever was I deserving of brotherhood with this gigantic summer sky. But for the moment no mention was made of this. Temporarily everything was forgiven me. I had to work out the morning's faith in me somewhere in the future. And everything around was dizzily hopeful, like a law in accordance with which no one need long remain under obligations of *this* sort.

I got my ticket without any difficulty and took my seat in the train. There was not long to wait before it left. And there I was again rolling along from Berlin to Marburg, but this time, as distinct from the first, I was travelling by day, my expenses paid, and—I was a completely new person. I rode in comfort on the money I had borrowed from V——, and the picture of my rooms at Marburg kept rising up in my mind.

Opposite me with their backs towards the engine, smoking, there rocked in a row: a man in a pince-nez which was waiting its chance to slip off his nose into the paper he was holding close, a clerk from the forestry department with a game-bag over his shoulder and a rifle at the bottom of the luggage-rack, and someone else and someone else still. They embarrassed me no more than the Marburg room which I could see. The nature of my silence hypnotised them. Occasionally I broke it intentionally to prove its power over them. It was understood. It was travelling with me, on the journey I was attached to its person and bore its stamp, one familiar to everybody from his own experience. Otherwise it would seem my neighbours would not have recompensed me with a silent participation, because I was treating them more in a polite offhand way than in a generally friendly one, and was more posing without a pose than sitting in the compartment. There was more kindliness and horse-sense in the carriage than cigar and engine smoke, ancient towns sped up to meet us and the furnishings of my Marburg room flashed into my mind from time to time. And for what particular reason?

About two weeks before the advent of the sisters a muddle had been made which was of considerable importance to me. I was the speaker in both seminars. My papers came off well. They met with approbation.

I was pressed to develop my arguments in greater detail and to deliver them again at the end of the summer semester. I jumped at the idea and set to work with redoubled zeal.

But from my very ardour an experienced observer would have said that I would never make a learned man. I lived through the learning of a subject much more intensely than the theme warranted. Some sort of vegetable pondering was implanted in me. Its characteristic lay in the fact that any secondary conception unrolling excessively in my argument, would begin to demand nourishment and care, and when, under its influence, I turned to books, I was drawn to them not from any disinterested attraction for knowledge, but for literary quotations to its advantage. In spite of the fact that my work was accomplished with the aid of logic, imagination, paper and ink, I liked it best of all because the more I wrote the more it became overgrown with a constantly thickening ornamentation of bookish citations and comparisons. But since a time-limit compelled me at a given moment to renounce written extracts and as a substitute simply to leave my authors open at the places I needed, a time arrived when the theme of my work materialised and could be reviewed at a glance from the threshold of the room. It lay outstretched across the room rather like a tree-fern which spreads its leafy coils over the table, the divan and the windowsill. To disorder them meant to break the thread of my argument, but a complete tidying up would be equivalent to burning an uncopied manuscript. The landlady had been strictly forbidden to lay a hand on them. Towards the end my room was not even cleaned. And when I saw a picture of my room on the journey I really saw my philosophy in its entirety and also its probable fate.

VI

I did not recognise Marburg on my arrival. The hill had grown and looked pinched, the town shrivelled and blackened.

My landlady opened the door. Looking me up and down from head to foot she asked that in the future I should give due warning to herself or her daughter in such cases. I answered that I had not been able to warn her beforehand because I had found it urgently necessary to visit Berlin without returning home. She gave me an even more mocking look. My sudden appearance without any things from the other end of Germany as though from an evening walk was beyond her comprehension. It struck her as an unfortunate fabrication. Shaking her head she handed me two letters. One was a sealed letter, the other a local postcard.

The letter was from a girl cousin from St. Petersburg who had unexpectedly turned up at Frankfurt. She wrote that she was on her way to Switzerland and would be three days in Frankfurt. The card, a third of which was covered in an impersonally neat handwriting, was signed by another hand only too familiar from signatures at the end of university notices, Cohen's hand. It was an invitation to dinner next Sunday.

Approximately the following exchange took place between the landlady and myself in German: "What is to-day?" "Saturday." "I won't be in for tea. Yes, and while I remember. I'm going to Frankfurt to-morrow. Please wake me in time for the first train." "But if I'm not mistaken, the *Herr Geheimrat* . . ." "Doesn't matter, I'll manage." "But that's impossible. At the *Herr Geheimrat's* they sit down to dinner at twelve o'clock, and you . . ." But there was something unseemly in this solicitude. With an expressive glance at the old woman I passed into my own room.

I sat on the bed in a state of abstraction which probably did not last more than a minute, then mastering the wave of uncalled-for self-pity I went down to the kitchen for a brush and pan. Flinging off my jacket and rolling up my sleeves I began clearing up the plant's ramifications. Half an hour later the room looked as if I were leaving and not even the books from the university library spoilt its tidiness. Neatly tying them in four piles so that they would be ready to hand when I was passing the library, I kicked them far under the bed. At this moment the landlady knocked at the door. She had come to tell me the exact hour of to-morrow's train in the time-table. At the sight of the change which had taken place she stopped short and suddenly, shaking her skirts, jacket and cap like feathers ruffled in a ball, she floated towards me on the air in a state of fluttering stupefaction. She put out her hand and congratulated me woodenly and ceremoniously on the completion of my difficult work. I did not feel like disillusioning her a second time. I left her in her gracious error.

Then I had a wash and went on to the balcony as I was drying myself. It was getting dark. Rubbing my neck on the towel I gazed into the distance which joined Ockershausen and Marburg. I could no longer remember how I had looked in that direction on the evening of my arrival. It was the end, the end! The end of philosophy, that is, the end of whatever thought I had entertained about it.

Like my fellow-travellers in the compartment, it would have to take into account that every love is a crossing over into a new faith.

VII

It was a wonder I didn't leave for home then. The value of the town lay in its school of philosophy. I had no further use for it. But another became manifest.

There exists the psychology of the creative genius, the problems of poetry. Yet in all art its conception in particular is experienced more directly than anything else and on this point there is no need to indulge in guesswork.

We cease to recognise reality. It appears in some new form. This form appears to be a quality inherent in it, and not in us. Apart from this quality everything in the world has its name. It alone is new and without name. We try to give it a name. The result is art.

The clearest, most memorable and important fact about art is its conception, and the world's best creations, those which tell of the most diverse things, in reality describe their own birth. I understood this for the first time in all its magnitude during the period I have described.

Though nothing occurred in my explanations with

V—— which could change my position, they were accompanied by surprises which resembled happiness. I was in despair, she comforted me. But her slightest touch was such bliss that it washed away in an exultant wave the bitterness of her definite refusal, which I heard so clearly and which could not be changed.

The day's events were like a rapid and noisy running to and fro. All the time we seemed to be flying at full speed into gloom and, without getting back our breath, rushing out again like an arrow. And so, without once stopping to look about us, we were at least twenty times that day in the crowded hold where the galley of time is set in motion. This was precisely that grown-up world of which I had been so furiously jealous from my earliest years when I was in love with V——, a schoolboy in love with a schoolgirl.

Returning to Marburg, I found myself separated, not from the little girl I had known for six years, but from the woman I had seen in the several seconds after her refusal. My hands and shoulders did not belong to me any more. Like someone else's limbs they begged me for those fetters which bind a man to general everyday doings. Because without irons I could no longer think of her either, and loved only in irons, only as a prisoner, only for the cold sweat in which beauty rids itself of its obligations. Every thought of her momentarily fitted me into that communal chorale which fills the world with a forest of movements which have been recorded with inspiration, a forest of movements like a battle, a penal servitude, a medieval hell or a trade. I mean something which children do not know and which I shall call the sense of the actual.

At the beginning of Safe Conduct I said that at times love raced the sun. I had in mind that manifestation of feeling which each morning outstripped everything around with the certainty of tidings, that had just been confirmed for the hundredth time. In comparison with these even the sunrise took on the character of town gossip which was still in need of confirmation. In other words, I had in mind the manifestation of a power which counter-balanced the manifestation of the world.

If, equipped with the necessary knowledge, ability and leisure, I decided now to write an aesthetic of creativity I would build it up on two conceptions, the conception of power and the conception of the symbol. I would point out that, as distinct from science which takes nature in a dissection of the pillar of light, art concerns itself with life as the ray of power *passes through it*. The conception of power I would take in that same widest sense in which it is taken by theoretical physics, with this difference only, that the subject under discussion would not be the principle of power but its voice, its presence. I would make it clear that within the framework of self-consciousness power is called feeling.

When we imagine that in Tristan, Romeo and Juliet and other memorials powerful passion is portrayed, we undervalue the subject matter. Their theme is wider than that powerful theme. Their theme is the theme of power itself.

And it is from this theme that art is born. It is more one-sided than people think. It cannot be directed at will where one wants like a telescope. Focussed on a reality which feeling has displaced, art is a record of this displacement. It copies from nature. How does nature get into this state of displacement? Details attain clarity, losing independence of meaning. Each detail can be replaced by another. Any one is precious. Any one chosen at random serves as evidence of the state which envelops the whole of transposed reality.

When the features of this state are transferred to paper, the characteristics of life become the characteristics of creation. The latter strike one more sharply than the former. They have been studied better. They have their terminology. They are called techniques.

Art is as realistic as activity and as symbolic as fact. It is realistic since it has not itself invented metaphor but discovered it in nature and reproduced it faithfully. The figurative meaning also means nothing separately, but refers to the general spirit of all art, in the same way as, taken singly, the parts of reality which feeling has displaced have no meaning.

And it is through the figure of its traction that art is symbolic. Its single symbol in the brightness and interchangeability of its images is characteristic of the whole. The interchangeability of images is an indication of the condition in which the parts of reality are independent of each other. The interchangeability of images, that is, art, is the symbol of power.

Properly speaking, only power needs the language of material proofs. The other means of perception are durable without being noted down. They lead straight to the visual analogies of light: to the number, the exact meaning, the idea. But one cannot imagine power to oneself, the fact of power, power lingering only in the moment of its manifestation, except in the two-fold language of images, that is, the language of accompanying features.

The direct speech of feeling is allegorical and cannot be replaced by anything.[5]

[5] In case of misunderstanding I would remind the reader. I am not speaking of the material contents of art, nor of the aspects of its completion, but of the meaning of its inception, of its place in life. Separate images by themselves are visual and are created on the analogy of light. The separate words of art, like all conceptions, exist by virtue of perception. But the word of the whole art which does not lend itself to quotation consists in the movement of the allegory itself and this word speaks symbolically of power.—Author's Note.

I went to see my cousin in Frankfurt, and also my people who had meanwhile arrived in Bavaria. My brother visited me and then my father. But I hardly noticed all this. I was completely taken up with writing poetry. Day and night and whenever a chance offered I wrote about the sea, about dawn, about the southern rain, about the hard coal of the Harz.

One day I was particularly engrossed in it. It was one of those nights which make their way with difficulty to the nearest fence and, completely exhausted, hang over the ground in fumes of weariness. There was not a breath of wind. Indeed the only sign of life was the black profile of the sky leaning weakly against the hedge. And another. The strong scent of flowering tobacco plants and stocks with which the earth called out in reply to this lassitude. To what can one not liken the sky on such a night! The large stars—like an evening reception, the milky way—like a great society. But the chalky daubs of the diagonally outstretched spaces remind one even more of a flower-bed at night. Here there are heliotropes and metioles. They were watered in the evening and pushed over sideways. Flowers and stars are so close together that it looks as though the sky came under the watering-can too and now the stars and white-speckled grasses are not to be torn apart.

I wrote with intense absorption, and a different dust from before settled on my table. The former, the philosophical dust had collected from schism. I had trembled for the completeness of my effort. Now I did not rub off the dust, simply for comradeship, out of sympathy with the rubble on the Giessen road. And on the far side of the oilcloth like a star in the sky, shone a long-unwashed tea glass.

Suddenly I got up, sweating from this idiotic liquefaction of everything and began pacing the room. "What a swinish trick!" I thought. "As if he has not remained a genius to me, as if I am breaking with *him!* It's nearly three weeks since his card and my base hiding from him! I must explain myself. But how?"

I remembered how pedantic and strict he was. "*Was ist Apperzepzion?*" he would ask a non-specialising examination candidate, and on his translating from Latin that it means . . . *durchfassen* (to grasp): "*Nein, das heisst durchfallen, mein Herr.*" (No, it means to plough), would be the reply.

In his seminars they used to read the classics. He would interrupt the reading and ask what the author was getting at. He expected the meaning to be expounded precisely in its essentials, in military fashion. Not only vagueness but anything merely approaching the truth instead of the exact truth was his abhorrence.

He was a little deaf in the right ear. I sat next to him on this particular side to expound my lesson from Kant. He let me get under way and lose myself in the argument, then when I was least expecting it dropped his customary: "*Was meint der Alte?*" (What does the old man mean?) I don't remember what it was, but let us suppose that according to the multiplication table of ideas the answer was as for five times five "Twenty-five," I answered. He frowned and made a gesture with his hand. This was followed by a slightly different version of the reply which displeased him with its tentativeness. It is easy to guess that while he jabbed into space to call up people who knew, my reply was varied with a growing complexity. So far it was still a matter of two and a half tens or roughly half a hundred divided by two. And the growing divergence of the answer annoyed him more and more. But no one could make up his mind to repeat what I had said first, after his disdainful look. Then with a gesture which might be interpreted as "to the rescue, Kamchatka!" [6] he turned to others. And: sixty-two, a hundred and eight, two hundred and fourteen —thundered around happily. Lifting his hands he hardly took in the storm of exultant mistakes and turning to me quietly and dryly repeated my own reply. A new storm broke out in my defence. When he had made it all out he looked me up and down, shook me by the shoulder and asked where I came from and how many terms I had been with them. Then snorting and frowning, he asked me to continue to a perpetual undertone of: "*Sehr echt, sehr richtig; Sie merken wohl? Ja, ja; ach, ach, der Alte!*" (That's right, that's right; do you follow? Ah, ah, the old man!) And I remembered a lot.more.

Well how was one to approach such a man? What could I say to him. "Verse?" he would drawl, "Verse!" Had he not studied human lack of talent and its subterfuges sufficiently? "Verse."

IX

Probably all this took place in July because the lime trees were in bloom. Bursting through the diamonds of the waxen blooms as through a burning-glass, the sun burnt the dusty leaves in little black rings.

I had often passed the exercise-ground before. At noon dust hovered above it from the battering pile-driver and a muffled shuddering clatter could be heard. The soldiers were taught there and during the hours of instruction loafers would take up their stand in front of the square—

[6] Kamchatka, the peninsula in the far east of Siberia, was jokingly referred to as the back of beyond, and so in Russian schools its name came to be given to the back bench where the worst members of the class used to sit.—*Translator's Note.*

boys from the sausage shops with trays on their shoulders and school-children. And certainly here was something worth gazing at. Scattered over the whole field in pairs rotund statues, rather like cockerels in sacks, sprang at each other and pecked. The soldiers wore padded jackets and headpieces of metal network. They were learning to fence.

The sight meant nothing new to me. I had had my fill of it during the course of the summer.

But on the morning after the night I have just described, as I was walking into the town and came level with the field, I suddenly remembered that not more than an hour ago I had seen this field in a dream.

Still having decided nothing about Cohen I went to bed at daybreak, slept through the morning, and just before waking up I dreamt of this field. It was a dream about the next war, self-evident, as the mathematicians would say, and unavoidable.

It has long been observed that however much the military regulations insist on a state of war, being concerned with companies and squadrons, thought in peacetime cannot effect the transition from the premises to the deduction. Daily, pale *chasseurs* dusty to their very eyebrows and dressed in faded uniforms marched round below Marburg as it was impossible to pass in ranks through the town on account of its narrowness. But the most that could enter one's head at the sight of them would be the stationers' shops where the same *chasseurs* were sold in sheets with a little gum-arabic thrown in for every dozen bought.

In my dream it was a different matter. There impressions were not bounded by the requirements of habit. There colours moved and came to a conclusion.

I dreamt I saw a desolate field and something told me it was—Marburg under siege. There filed past pushing barrows in front of them pale, lanky *Nettel'beki*. It was some dark hour of the day which does not exist in real life. The dream was in the style of Frederick with trenches and earthworks. On the battery heights people with telescopes could just be descried. They were wrapped in a physically tangible silence which does not exist in real life. It pulsated in the air like a porous earthy blizzard and did not stand still but was *being consummated,* as if it was constantly being added to by spadefuls. It was the saddest dream of any I have ever seen. Probably I wept in my sleep. The affair with V—— was deeply lodged in me. I had a sound heart. It worked well. Working at night it caught up the most accidental and random of the day's impressions. And so here it caught at the exercise ground and its push was sufficient to bring the mechanism of the exercise ground into motion and the dream-vision itself in its circular movement, beat out quietly: "I am a dream-vision of war."

I don't know why I was making for the town but I was as heavy at heart as if my head were full of earth which was intended for some sort of fortification.

It was the dinner-hour. None of my friends turned out to be in the university. The seminar reading-room was empty. The private houses of the little town stepped up to it from below. The heat was merciless. Here and there at the windowsills came glimpses of drowning people with collars crumpled to one side. Behind them glimmered the half-light of front rooms. From inside entered lean female martyrs in dressing-gowns boiled through on the chest as if in laundry coppers. I returned home, deciding to go along the top, where by the castle wall there were many shady villas.

Their gardens rested in layers on the smithy-like heat and only the rose-stalks, as if just from the anvil, bent proudly over the slow blue flame. I longed for a little mews which descended abruptly behind one of these villas. There was some shade there. I knew that. I decided to turn down it and have a rest. To my great amazement, in the same stupor in which I had decided to turn into it I saw Professor Hermann Cohen there. He noticed me. My retreat was cut off.

My son is nearly seven. When he does not understand a French sentence and merely guesses its meaning from the context in which it is made, he says: "I understand it not from the words but *because.*" Fullstop. Not because of this and that but: "I *understood* because."

I will make use of his terminology in naming the mind which *leads one to a given point,* as distinct from the mind which takes one for a healthy constitutional, the *casual mind.*

Cohen had such a casual mind. It was rather frightening to chat with him and to walk along with him was no joke. Leaning on a walking-stick the real spirit of mathematical physics advanced by your side, with frequent stops, pacing with approximately the same gait, step by step assembling its basic propositions. This university professor in his bulky overcoat and soft hat was filled at a certain temperature with the precious essence which had long ago been packed into the heads of the Galileos, the Newtons, the Leibnizs and the Pascals.

He did not like talking as he walked and merely listened to the chatter of those he met, never even in its flow on account of the steepness of the Marburg pavements. He paced along, listening, then would stop suddenly, pronounce something caustic on the subject he had heard, and, pushing off with his stick against the pavement, continued the walk to the next aphoristic breathing-space.

Our conversation proceeded on lines like these. A reference to my negligence only made it seem worse—he gave me to understand this in a deadly fashion without a word, adding nothing to the mocking silence of the stick pressed firmly into the stone. My plans interested him. He did not commend them. In his opinion I should remain with them until the exam. for my doctorate, take it, and only then return home to take the public Russian exam., with the possible intention of returning subsequently to the West and of establishing myself there. I thanked him with great warmth for his hospitality. But my gratitude told him much less than the attraction which Moscow held for me. From the way in which I put it he sensed a falsity and unintelligibility which outraged him because, on account of life's puzzling lack of duration, he could not bear those of its puzzles which curtailed it artificially. And, containing his irritation, he descended slowly from flag to flag, waiting in case the man would ultimately state his case after so many trifling and wearisome platitudes.

But how could I tell him that I was throwing philosophy over completely, that I meant to finish in Moscow like the majority, just for the sake of finishing, and that a subsequent return to Marburg did not even enter my head. To him, whose farewell words before his retirement, were on his faithfulness to great philosophy, delivered to the university in such a way that among the benches, where there were many young listeners, handkerchiefs gleamed.

X

In the beginning of August my people crossed from Bavaria into Italy and asked me to come to Pisa. My money was running short and hardly enough remained for my return to Moscow. One evening, which I foresaw would be followed by many similar ones in the future, I was sitting with G—— on the terrace we frequented and was complaining about the sorry state of my finances. He was discussing it. At different times he had experienced poverty in all seriousness, and just during these periods he had wandered a good deal about the world. He had been in England and Italy and knew means of living almost free while travelling about. His plan was that on the remainder of my money I ought to make a trip to Venice and Florence and then go to my parents for feeding up and a new subsidy for the return journey, which I might not even find necessary if I was miserly with what I had left. He began putting figures on paper and submitted a really very modest total.

The head waiter in the cafe was a friend to us all. He knew the innermost thoughts of each of us. When in the white heat of my experiment my brother came to visit me and embarrassed me at my work in the daytime, the incredible man discovered in him a rare gift for billiards and got him so interested in the game that he left every morning to perfect his talent in his company, leaving my room at my disposal for the whole day.

He took the liveliest part in the discussion of the Italian plan. Constantly leaving us he would return to tap G——'s estimate with a pencil and find even it not economical enough.

He came running back after one of these absences with a thick reference book under his arm, placed a tray with three glasses of strawberry punch on the table, and opening the book ran through it twice from end to end. In the whirlwind of pages finding the one he wanted he announced that I must start that same night on the express at a few minutes past three, in token of which he invited us to drink with him to my trip.

I did not waiver long. It was quite true, I thought, following the line of his arguments. I had received my discharge from the university. The part-payments were in order. It was half-past eleven. To wake the landlady—no great sin. Plenty of time for packing and more. That settled it—I was going.

He was filled with such delight that it looked as if it was he who would see Basle to-morrow. "Listen," he said, coming nearer and gathering up the empty glasses. "Let's look closely at one another, that's a custom we have. It may be useful, you never know." I burst out laughing in answer and assured him that it was unnecessary because it had long ago been done and I would never forget him.

We took leave of each other, I followed G—— out, and the dull ring of the nickel-plated cutlery died away behind us, as it seemed to me then, forever.

Several hours later having talked our heads off and tramped the little town till we were stupid, quickly using up the small stock of our streets, G—— and I descended to the district adjoining the station. A mist surrounded us. We stood motionless in it like cattle at a watering-place and smoked tenaciously with that silent dullwittedness from which cigarettes tend to go out.

Very gradually day began to dawn. Dew held the gardens tightly in goose-flesh. Beds of satin seedlings burst out of the gloom. Suddenly in this stadium of dawnlight the town was silhouetted entire on its present height. People were asleep there. Churches, a castle and a university were there. But they still melted into the grey sky like a clump of cobwebs on a damp mop. It even seemed to me that standing out slightly, the town began to flow like the trace of a breath, caught in a few paces away from the window. "Come on, it's time," said G——.

It was growing light. We walked quickly over the stone platform. Fragments of an approaching roar flew in our faces like stones. The train raced up, I embraced my friend, and throwing my case up jumped on to the running-board. The stones in the concrete rolled shrieking, the door clicked, I pressed against the window. The train cut me clean away from everything I had experienced and, sooner than I expected, there flashed by, jostling each other—the Lahn, the level-crossing, the road and my recent home. I pulled at the window-frame. It wouldn't open. Suddenly with a clatter it fell down of its own accord. I put out my head as far as I could. The carriage was rocking on a violent bend and I couldn't see anything. Farewell philosophy, farewell youth, farewell Germany!

XI

Six years passed. When everything was forgotten, when the war had dragged itself out and ended, and the Revolution had begun, into the low twilight scarcely two stories high along the snow out of the gloom there crawled and rang out through the flat an untimely telephone bell. "Who is it?" I asked. "G——," came the reply. I was not even amazed that it was amazing. "Where are you?" I squeezed out untimely. He answered. Another absurdity. The place turned out to be next to us across the yard. He was ringing up from an hotel taken over to house the People's Commissariat of Education. In a minute I was sitting with him. His wife had not changed a bit. I had not known his children before.

But this is what was unexpected. It turned out that he had lived all these years in the world like everyone else, and though abroad, nevertheless still under the shadow of the same gloomy war for the liberation of small countries. I found out he had not long ago come from London. And he was either in the Party or an enthusiastic supporter of it. He was working. At the removal of the Government to

Moscow he had automatically been moved with the relevant section of the P.C.E.'s apparatus. That's why he was our neighbour. And that was all.

And I had rushed to him as to a Marburger. Not of course so as to begin life with his aid afresh from that far-off misty dawn when we stood in the gloom like cattle at a watering-place—and this time more carefully, without a war, as best we could. O, of course not for that! But knowing in advance that to recapture this was unthinkable, I rushed to make certain why it was unthinkable in my life.

.   .   .   .   .   .

Later I was fortunate enough to visit Marburg once more. I spent two days there in February of '23. I was going there with my wife but did not have the foresight to bring it near to her. In this I was at fault before both. But it was hard even for me. I had seen Germany before the War and now saw it after. What had happened in the world became manifest to me in the most terrifying exposition. It was during the period of the Ruhr occupation. Germany was starving and freezing, deceived by nothing, deceiving no one, with a hand stretched out to the times as for alms (a gesture uncharacteristic of her) and went on crutches to a man.

To my surprise I found my landlady among the living. At the sight of me she and her daughter fluttered their hands wildly. They were both sitting in the same places as eleven years ago and were sewing when I appeared. The room was to let. They opened the door for me. I would not have recognised it if it had not been for the road from Ockershausen to Marburg. That could be seen from the window as before. And it was winter. The untidiness of the empty chilled room and the bare willows on the

77

horizon—all this was unusual. The landscape which had once pondered too long on the Thirty Years' War had ended by foreboding war for itself. On leaving the town I went into a cakeshop and sent the two women a large nutty *torte.*

And now of Cohen. We could not see Cohen. Cohen was dead.

XII

And so—stations, stations, stations. Stations flying away to the end of the train like stone butterflies.

There was a sabbath calm in Basle, so that one could hear the swallows bustling and rustling against the cornices with their wings. The glowing walls rolled like the apples of eyes under the overhanging blackcherry-tiled rooves. The whole town was blinking and protruding them like eyelashes. And in the same earthenware fire with which the wild vine burnt on the houses, the baked gold of the primitives burnt in the cool clean museum.

"*Zwei francs vierzig centimes*"—a peasant woman in the costume of the canton pronounced with surprising clearness, but the place where the two linguistic reservoirs flow into one another was not yet here, but to the right beyond the lowhanging roof, south of it, along the hot free expanse of the Federal azure and uphill all the way. Somewhere by St. Gotthard and—in the depths of night, people were talking.

And I slept through such a place, worn out with the nightly vigils of my forty-eight-hour journey. The one night when I ought not to have slept—almost like some "Simon, sleepest thou?"—and it would be forgiven me. But still for moments I did waken and stood by the window for shamefully short periods, "for their eyes were heavy." And then . . .

All around there noised a world reunion of heights motionlessly crowded together. Aha, so while I had been dozing and while, letting out whistle after whistle, we had screwed ourselves upwards in a spiral through the cold smoke from tunnel to tunnel, air excelling our natural air by three thousand metres had already succeeded in surrounding us?

An impenetrable blackness reigned but echo filled it with a protuberant sculpture of sounds. The precipices conversed loudly without shyness, washing over the bones of the earth like old wives. Everywhere, everywhere, the streams slandered, gossiped and trickled along. One could easily guess how they were hung about the sheer drops and were let down like spun threads into the vale below. And from above overhanging jags leapt on to the train and, settling themselves on the carriage roofs, called to each other waving their legs and abandoned themselves to the free ride.

But sleep was overtaking me and I fell into an impermissible dozing on the threshold of the snows, by the blind Oedipus' whites of the Alps, on the summit of the planet's demoniac perfection. At the height of the kiss which, like Michelangelo's Night, it plants here in self-love on its own shoulder.

When I woke up the clean Alpine morning was looking in at the windows. Some sort of accident like a fall on the line had stopped the train. We were asked to change into another. We went along the rails uphill. The linen ribbon twisted through disjointed panoramas as if the road was constantly being pushed round a corner like something stolen. A barefoot Italian boy just like the ones on chocolate boxes carried my things. Somewhere not far off his flock was lowing. The tinkling of little bells fell in lazy shakes and brandishings. The gad-flies sucked the music. Probably its skin was creeping with cold. The daisies were wafting sweet perfume and the pouring from the empty to the still more void of the invisibly splashing waters on all sides never ceased for a moment.

The results of not giving full measure to sleep were not slow in showing themselves. I was half a day in Milan and did not memorise it. Only the cathedral, constantly changing its aspect as I approached it through the town, depending on the cross-roads from which it was subsequently disclosed, impressed itself dimly upon me. Like a melting glacier it grew up again and again on the deep blue perpendicular of the August heat and seemed to nourish the innumerable Milan cafes with ice and water. When at last a narrow platform placed me at its foot and I craned my head, it slid into me with the whole choral murmur of its pillars and turrets, like a plug of snow down the jointed column of a drainpipe.

Still, I could hardly keep on my feet and the main thing I promised to give myself on reaching Venice was a sound sleep.

XIII

When I came out of the station which had a provincial pent-roof in some kind of Excise-cum-Customshouse style, something smooth slipped softly by my wet feet. Something malignantly dark like swill and touched by two or three gleams from the stars. It rose and fell almost imperceptibly and was like a painting dark with age in a swaying frame. I did not at once understand that this image of Venice was Venice. That I was in it and that I was not dreaming this.

The canal in front of the station went in a blind tube round the corner towards the furthermost wonders of this floating gallery on the cloaca. I hastened to the landing-stage of the cheap boats which here took the place of trams.

The launch sweated and puffed, wiped its nose and swallowed hard, and, in the same serene smoothness along which dragged its submerged moustaches, the palaces of the Grand Canal swam along the semicircle which gradually retreated before us. They call them palaces and they could call them by finer names, but still no words can give any idea of their carpets of coloured marble, let steeply down into the nocturnal lagoon, as into the arena of a medieval tourney.

There is a special Christmas tree East, the East of the Pre-Raphaelites. There is the presentation of the starry night according to the legend of the worship of the Magi. There is the age-old Christmas relief: the top of a gilded walnut sprinkled with blue paraffin. There are words: *Khalva* and Chaldea, Magi and magnesium, India and indigo. To these should be borne both the colouring of Venice at night and its water reflections.

As if to stress the nutty gamut better to the Russian ear, they call out on the barge as it stops now on one side now on the other, to pick up the passengers: "*Fondaco dei turchi! Fondaco dei tedeschi!*" But it seems the names of the landing-stages having nothing in common with warehouses, but are a final reminiscence of the caravan-warehouses once built here by the Turkish and German merchants.

I don't remember before which of these Vendraminis, Grimanis, Korneros, Foscaris and Loredanos I saw the first gondola, or the first to surprise me. But it was already on the other side of the Rialto. It slipped noiselessly into the canal out of a side-turning and cutting across began to moor by the nearest palace portal. It was as if it had been brought from the backdoor to the front on the round belly of a slowly rolling wave. It left a groove behind it, full of dead rats and floating melonskins. In front of it ran the deserted moonlit extent of the wide water-bridge. It was

81

enormous like a female, enormous as if everything which is perfect in form and incommensurable with the place its body takes up in space. Its bright crested halberd sped lightly along the sky borne aloft by the wave's round brow. The gondolier's black silhouette ran along the stars as lightly. And the cowl of the cabin was lost as if pressed into the water in the hollow between stern and prow.

I had decided beforehand from G——'s accounts of Venice that it would be best of all to settle in the neighbourhood of the Academy. And I did this. I can't remember whether I crossed the bridge to the left shore or whether I stayed on the right. I remember a tiny square. It was surrounded by similar palaces to those on the canal, only they were greyer and sterner. And they leant on dry land.

On the moonlit square people stood, strolled and half lay. There were not many and they seemed to be draping it with moving, slightly moving and unmoving bodies. It was an exceptionally quiet night. One pair I noticed. Without turning their heads towards each other and delighting in their mutual silence, they gazed intently into the distance of the further shore. Probably they were servants in the *palazzo*, resting after their work. First I was attracted by the quiet bearing of the waiter, his trim greying hair, the grey of his jacket. There was something un-Italian in them. They gave off a northern breeze. Then I saw his face. I thought I had seen it before and I could not remember where it was.

Going up to him with my suitcase I told him about my need of a lodging in imperfect phraseology which I had acquired after past efforts to read Dante in the original. He heard me out politely, thought a moment and asked something of a waitress standing near. She shook her head in the negative. He took out a watch with a lid, looked at the time, closed it, pushed it back in his waistcoat and coming out of his meditation, beckoned me with a nod to follow him. We turned the corner from the moonlit façade and it was pitch dark.

We walked along stony mews no wider than corridors. Now and again they lifted us on to short bridges of hump-backed stone. Then on either side stretched the dirty sleeves of the lagoon where the water stood in such straits that it looked like a Persian carpet rolled up, just squeezed into the bottom of a crooked drawer.

On the hump-back bridges we met passers-by and long before the Venetian woman appeared the frequent tapping of her shoes on the flagstones of the quarter heralded her approach.

High above, across the crevices black as pitch in which we were wandering, the night sky shone and kept withdrawing somewhere. As if along the entire Milky Way the fluff of dandelion seeds was passing, and as if simply to let through another column of this moving light, the mews drew apart making squares and crossways. And surprised by the strange familiarity of the man I had met, I talked to him in very imperfect Italian and fell from pitch to fluff, from fluff to pitch, seeking with his aid the cheapest possible lodging for the night.

But on the shores of the outlet to the open sea, different colours reigned and bustle took the place of silence. On the launches coming and going people crowded, and the oily black water glowed with a snowy dust, like beaten marble, breaking in the pestle of a fiercely working or abruptly jammed machine. And next to its bubbling the lamps buzzed brightly in the fruiterers' stalls, tongues chattered and fruit jumped in the senseless columns of some sort of underdone *compôtes*.

In one of the restaurant sculleries by the shore we were given useful directions. The address given led back to the

beginning of our pilgrimage. On our way there we re-
traced our whole journey. And so, when my escort installed
me in one of the lodging-houses near the *Campo Morosini*,
I felt as if I had just traversed a distance equal to the starry
sky of Venice in the opposite direction of its movement.
If I had then been asked what Venice is, I would have
said: "Light nights, tiny squares, and quiet people who
seem strangely familiar."

XIV

"Well, my friend"—my host roared loudly as if I were
deaf; he was a sturdy old man of about sixty, in a dirty
open shirt. "I'll fix you up like a relative." The blood rose
to his face, he measured me with his gaze from beneath
his brows, and placing his hands on the buckles of his
braces, drummed with his fingers on his hairy chest.
"Would you like some cold veal?" he bellowed without
softening his look, inferring nothing from my reply.

Probably he was a kindhearted man who was making
himself out a bogey, with a moustache *à la Radetski*. He
could remember the Austrian occupation and it soon came
out that he could speak German a little. But as he took
this tongue to be pre-eminently that of the non-com-
missioned officers of Dalmatia, my rapid pronunciation
made him reflect sadly on the decay of the German
language since the day when he was a soldier. Besides
which he probably had indigestion.

Getting up from behind the counter as if he were in
stirrups he shouted bloodthirstily somewhere and descended springily into the little yard where our acquaintance was maturing. Several little tables with dirty cloths
were standing there. "I felt myself friendly disposed
towards you as soon as you came in"—he squeezed out
malignantly, inviting me to be seated with a wave of his

hand, and himself sank into a chair two or three tables away from me. They brought me meat and beer.

The little courtyard served as a dining hall. The other lodgers if there were any had probably supped long ago and wandered away to their rest, and there was only a vile old man sitting on in the extreme corner of the eating arena, willingly agreeing with the host on every point on which he turned to him for confirmation.

Tucking in at the veal, I had already noticed once or twice the strange disappearance and reappearance of the moist pink slices on my plate. Apparently I was dozing. My eyelids stuck together.

As suddenly as in a fairy-tale a dear withered old woman appeared by the table, and my host informed her briefly of his savage philanthropy towards me, after which, going with her up a narrow staircase somewhere, I found myself alone, felt for the bed and without further thought, undressed in the dark and lay down.

I woke on a bright sunny morning after ten hours of continuous uninterrupted slumber. The impossible had been confirmed. I found myself in Venice. The sunbeams trotting like bright mites on the ceiling as in the cabin of a river-steamer, all told of this and of the fact that I would get up now and rush out to look around.

I examined the room in which I lay. On nails driven into the painted screen, hung skirts and blouses, a feather duster on a ring, and a beater caught on a nail by its plaiting. The windowsill was loaded with creams in tins. In a sweet box lay some dirty chalk.

Behind a curtain drawn across the whole length of the attic, the tap and rush of a bootbrush could be heard. That would be the cleaning of all the guest-house shoes in progress. To the noise was added a woman's hushings and a child's whispers. In the hushing woman I recognised my old woman of yesterday.

85

She was a distant relative of the landlord's and worked as a housekeeper for him. He had given me her little closet, but when I wanted this to be put right somehow, she herself asked me nervously not to meddle with their family affairs.

Before dressing, I stretched myself and looked round once again, and suddenly a momentary gift of clarity illumined the circumstances of the previous day. My friend yesterday reminded me of the head waiter at Marburg, the same one who had hoped to be of further use to me.

The probable effect of the suggestion implicit in his request was to exaggerate this likeness. And it was this which had been the reason for the instinctive preference which I felt for one of the people in the square out of all the others.

This discovery did not surprise me. There was nothing miraculous about it. Our most innocent "how-do-you-do's" and "good-byes" would have no meaning, if time were not threaded with the concord of life's accidents, that is, the haphazard events of the hypnosis of being.

xv

And so this happiness crossed my path too. I too was fortunate enough to find that one can go day after day to meet a piece of built-up space as one would go to meet a live personality.

From whatever side one walks up to the piazza a certain moment lies in wait at each approach, when one's breath comes fast, and one hastens one's step till one's feet begin to take one to meet it of their own accord. Whether from the direction of the mercerie or that of the telegraph office, at some point the road becomes a threshold and flinging out its own widely ruled air the square leads out as to a reception: the Campanile, the Cathedral, the Palace of the Doges and the three-sided gallery.

Gradually as one becomes attached to them, one inclines to the feeling that Venice is a town inhabited by buildings—by the four just mentioned and a few others like them. There is nothing figurative about this statement. The word the architects spoke in stone is so lofty that no rhetoric can stretch to its heights. And besides, it has become overgrown with the seashells of the age-old enthusiasm of travellers. The growing delight has ousted the last trace of declamation from Venice. There are no empty places left in the empty palaces. Everything is full of beauty.

When, before sitting down in the gondola hired to take them to the station, Englishmen linger for the last time on the piazza in postures which would be sincere at a leavetaking from a live person, you envy them the piazza all the more poignantly, because, as is well known, no European culture has approached the Italian so closely as the English.

XVI

Once, beneath these standard-bearing masts, entwined with generations as with golden threads, crowded three admirably interwoven centuries, and not far from the square in a motionless forest of ships the fleet of these ages dreamed. It looked as if it were continuing the planning of the city. Tackle jutted out from behind the attics, galleys peered, men moved in the same way on ships as on dry land. On a moonlit night some three-master, digging its rib against the street, enchained it with the deadly menace of its motionlessly unfurled impact. And bearing out this same grandeur, the frigates lay at anchor admiring from the roadway the quieter and loftier of the halls.

This fleet was very powerful by the standards of those days. Its size was amazing. In the fifteenth century its merchant ships, not counting the warships, already numbered about three and a half thousand, with seventy thousand sailors and craftsmen.

This fleet was Venice's unfeigned reality, the prosaic secret of its fairy-tale. Putting it paradoxically one could say that its rocking tonnage made up the firm ground of the town, its earthy foundation and its mercantile and prison subterraneous vault. In the toils of its rigging moped the imprisoned air. The fleet overpowered and oppressed. But, as in two vessels which are in communication with one another, from the shore in measure as the fleet oppressed there arose something which provided a counterbalancing ransom. To understand this is to understand how art deceives its customer.

The derivation of the word "pantaloons" is curious. Once, before its present meaning of trousers, it denoted a character in Italian comedy. But earlier still, in its original meaning "*pianta leone*" expressed the idea of Venetian triumph and meant: the erector of the lion (on the crest), that is, in other words, Venice the conqueress. Byron even mentions this in *Childe Harold*:

> "Her very byword sprung from victory,
> The 'Planter of the Lion,' which through fire
> And blood she bore o'er subject earth and sea."

Meanings change amazingly. When people get accustomed to horrors, these form the foundation for good style. Shall we ever understand how the guillotine could be temporarily made the decoration for a lady's brooch?

The emblem of the lion figured diversely in Venice. And so the slit for posting secret denunciations on the staircase of the Censors, next to the paintings of Veronese and Tintoretto, was carved in the semblance of a lion's maw. It is obvious how great a terror this "*bocca di leoni*" instilled in its contemporaries, and how, gradually, it was held to be a mark of ill-breeding to mention the persons so puzzlingly tumbling into the beautifully carved slit, on those occasions when the powers that be did not express vexation on the subject.

When art was erecting palaces for the enslavers, it was believed in. They thought it shared the general opinions of the day and in the future would bear witness to the general participation. But precisely this did not happen. The language of forgetfulness turned out to be the language of the palaces, and not at all the pantaloon language which had wrongly been ascribed to them. The pantaloon aims were forgotten, the palaces remained.

And Venetian painting remained. I was familiar from childhood with the savour of its hot strong springs from reproductions and imported museum preserves. But it was necessary to get to their birthplace to see as distinct from single pictures the painting itself, like a golden marsh, like one of the primitive pools of art.

XVII

I gazed at this spectacle more intently and more generally than any present formulation expresses it. I did not attempt to recognise in what I saw the tendencies which I am now interpreting. But the impressions themselves lay detached in my mind in the same shape as years went by, and I shall not stray from the truth in my compressed conclusion.

I saw what particular observation first strikes the painting instinct. The manner in which it is suddenly seized, what it becomes when they begin to see it. Once observed, nature opens out in the obedient expanse of a tale, and in this condition, sleepy, it is quietly borne on to the canvas. One must see Carpaccio and Bellini to understand the meaning of representation.

I found out later, what syncretism accompanies the flowering of craftsmanship, when at the attained identification of the artist and the painting element, it becomes impossible to say which of the three and for whose benefit reveals himself the more actively on the canvas—the executor, the thing executed or the subject of the execution. One must see Veronese and Titian to understand the meaning of craftsmanship.

Finally, not then sufficiently valuing these impressions, I found out how little a genius needs to burst out.

Who will believe this? The identification of the painting, the painter and the subject of the painting, or putting it more widely: an indifference to the immediacy of truth, is what infuriates him. As though this is a slap in the face of humanity in his person. And a storm enters his canvas, cleansing the chaos of workmanship with regulating blows of passion. One must see the Michelangelo of Venice—Tintoretto, to understand the meaning of genius, that is, of the artist.

XVIII

But in those days I did not enter into these finer points. In Venice at that time, and more powerfully still in Florence, or to be fully exact, during the winter immediately following my travels, in Moscow, other more specialised thoughts occurred to me.

The most outstanding thing which anyone carries away with him after an acquaintance with Italian art, is a sense of the tangible unity of our culture, in whatever form he may see it and whatever he may call it.

For instance, what a lot has been said about the paganism of the humanists, and in how many different ways—as concerning a natural and unnatural development. And to be sure the coinciding of the belief in the resurrection with the age of the Renaissance was an extraordinary phenomenon and a focal one for the whole culture of Europe. In the same way who has not noticed the anachronism often immoral in the treatment of canonical themes in all those "The Presentation," "The Ascension," "The Marriage of Cana" and "The Lord's Suppers" with their licentious splendours of the great social world?

And it was in just this lack of correspondence that the thousand-year-old peculiarity of our culture revealed itself to me.

Italy crystallised for me all that we unconsciously breathe in from our cradles. Her painting itself completed for me what I had to think out in this connection, and while I went day by day from collection to collection, it flung whole at my feet an observation decocted ultimately from paint.

I came to understand for instance that the Bible is not so much a book with a hard and fast text, as the notebook of humanity, and also what is the nature of everything eternal. That it is vital not when it is obligatory, but when it is amenable to all the comparisons with which the ages receding from it gaze back at it. I understood that the history of culture is the chain of equations in images, binding two by two the next unknown in turn with the known, and in addition this known, constant for the whole series, makes its appearance as legend, folded into the rudiments of tradition, yet the unknown, new each time—is the actual moment of the stream of culture.

And this what I was then interested in, what I then understood and loved.

I loved the living essence of historical symbolism, or, putting it another way, that instinct with the help of which we like Salangan swallows built the world—an enormous nest, put together from the earth and sky, life and death, and two times, the ready to hand and the defaulting. I understood that it was prevented from crumbling by the strength of its links, consisting in the transparent figurativeness of all its parts.

But I was young and did know that this does not embrace the genius' fate and his nature. I did not know that his being reposes in the experience of real biography and not in a symbolism refracted with images. I did not know that as distinct from the primitives, his roots lie in the rough directness of the moral instinct. His peculiarity alone is noteworthy. Although all the blazings-up of the moral affect play themselves out within the culture, the rioter always thinks his rioting rolls along the street beyond its boundary. I did not know that the iconoclast leaves alone the longest-lived images on those rare occasions when he is not born empty-handed.

When Pope Julius II expressed his displeasure on the score of the poor colouring of the Sistine Ceiling, Michelangelo, referring to this ceiling on which is represented the creation of the world with the appropriate figures, justified himself by remarking: "In those days men were not decked out in gold. The people represented here were not rich." There you have the thunder-like and infant language of this type.

Man arrives at the bounds of culture, melting in himself a subdued Savonarola. The unsubdued Savonarola breaks it.

XIX

On the evening before my departure there was a concert with illuminations on the piazza, which was an event that took place frequently there. The façades which surrounded it were decked from top to bottom with the points of the little lamps. The piazza was lit up on three sides with a whitish-black transparency. Under the open sky the faces of the audience glowed with a clarity which is characteristic of the baths, as in a covered, wonderfully illuminated hall. Suddenly from the ceiling of this imaginary ballroom fell a slight shower. But hardly had it begun when the rain as suddenly ceased. The reflection of the illumination simmered above the square in a coloured dimness. The bell-tower of St. Mark's cut like a red marble rocket into the rose mist which had risen in wreathes halfway up towards its summit. A little farther off dark-olive steams circled, and as in a fairy-tale the five-headed shell of the Cathedral hid within them. That side of the square looked like a deep-sea kingdom. On the Cathedral porch four steeds shone gold, which had galloped swiftly from Ancient Greece and had come to a halt here as though on the edge of a precipice.

When the concert was over, there could be heard the even shuffle of the mill-stone which had been turning before this along the circle of the gallery but had then been drowned by the music. This was the ring of loungers whose footsteps rang out and then melted together like the rush of skates on an ice-rink.

In the midst of the strollers the women passed quickly and angrily, rather threatening than scattering seduction. They turned their heads as they walked as if to ward off and annihilate. Their figures swaying invitingly, they quickly passed out of sight somewhere under the porticoes. When they turned, the funereally darkened face in the black Venetian kerchief stared at you. Their swift gait in the tempo of "allegro irato" corresponded strangely with the dark trembling of the illuminations, with the white scratches of its little diamond lights.

93

I have twice tried to express in poetry the sensation which for me is for ever linked up with Venice. In the night before I left I woke in the guest-house to the sound of an arpeggio on the guitar which broke off at the moment of waking. I hurried to the window beneath which water was splashing and began gazing intently into the distances of the nocturnal sky, as if a trace of the suddenly fading music might remain there. Judging from my gaze an onlooker would have said that in my semi-wakeful state I was looking to see if some new constellation had not risen above Venice, from a vaguely ready premonition about it, as about the Constellation of the Guitar.

PART THREE

I

IN WINTER TIME the chain of boulevards, behind their double curtains of blackened trees, dissected Moscow. In the houses fires gleamed yellow, like the starry circles of lemons cut in half. The snow-laden sky hung low above the trees and everything white around was tinted blue.

Along the boulevards ran poorly dressed young people, crouching as if to butt with their heads. I was acquainted with some of them, did not know the majority, but all of them together were my equals in age, that is, they were the numberless faces of my childhood.

People had just begun to call them by their patronymics, to endow them with rights and to initiate them into the secret of the words: to be in possession, to profit, to appropriate. They betrayed a hurry which deserves a more attentive investigation.

The world contains death and prevision. The unknown is dear to us, and what is known in advance is frightening, and every passion is a blind leap aside from the onrolling inevitable. Live species would have nowhere to exist and repeat themselves, if passion had nowhere to leap from that common road along which rolls that common time which is the time of the gradual disintegration of the universe.

But there is room for life to live and passion to leap, because there exists alongside the common time the unceasing endlessness of wayside regulations, undying in their reproduction, and because every new generation makes its appearance as one of these.

Bowed as they ran, young people hurried through the snowstorm, and although each had his own reasons for hurrying, still, they were spurred on by something they all had in common more than by their personal considerations, and this was their historical integrity, that is, the return of that passion with which humanity had just entered into them, rescued from the common road, for the countless time avoiding the end.

And to shield them from the duality of a flight through the unavoidable and so that they would not go mad, would not abandon what was begun and would not hang themselves over the whole globe, behind the trees along all the boulevards a power stood on guard, a power terribly tried and experienced, a power which followed them with wise eyes. Art stood behind the trees, an art which discriminates so wonderfully in us that we are always at a loss to know from what non-historical worlds it has brought its skill to see history in silhouette. It stood behind the trees and bore a terrible resemblance to life, and it endured this likeness, as the portraits of wives and mothers are endured in the laboratories of the learned, those dedicated to the natural sciences, that is, to the gradual puzzling out of death.

What kind of art was this? It was the young art of Scriabin, Blok, Komissarzhevsky, Biely—the leading art, enthralling, original. And it was so astounding that not only did it not awake any thoughts of a change, but on the contrary, one wanted to repeat it and make it all the more lasting from its very beginning, only to repeat it more swiftly, more warmly and more completely. One desired to

96

repeat it at a gulp, which would be inconceivable without passion, then passion leapt aside, and along this track something new was made. But the new did not arise from a change of the old, which is the generally accepted way of thinking, but quite the opposite, it arose from an exultant reproduction of the pattern. This was the nature of the art. And what was the nature of the generation?

Boys who were about my own age had been thirteen in 1905 and were nearly twenty-two before the war. Both their critical ages coincided with the two red dates of their country's history. Their childhood, adolescence and their calling-up at coming of age were immediately fastened to an epoch of transition. The whole bulk of our time is threaded through with their nerves and is politely abandoned by them for the use of the aged and of children.

When I returned from abroad it was the Centenary of the Napoleonic Invasion of 1812. The railroad from Brestsk was renamed the Alexander. The stations were whitewashed, the watchmen at the bells were dressed in clean blouses. The station hall at Kubinka was stuffed with flags and at the doors a reinforced guard stood on duty. Near by a grand parade was taking place and for this event the platform burnt with a bright heap of porous sand which had not yet been stamped down everywhere.

This did not call up in the passengers memories of the events commemorated. The jubilee decorations exhaled the primary peculiarity of the reign—an indifference to native history. And if the festivities were reflected in anything, it was not in the course of thoughts but in the course of the train because it was detained longer than was expected at stations and was stopped more than usual in the fields by signals.

III

We made each other's acquaintance in the constrained circumstances of group prejudice. A long time before that Y. Anisimov had shown me his poems in the *Sadok Sudei*, as a poet shows off another poet. But this was in the Epigone circle "*Lyrika*." The Epigones were not ashamed of their sympathies, and in their circle Mayakovsky was discovered as a phenomenon soon to fulfil great promise, as a giant.

Besides this, I discovered in the Novator group "Centrifugue" in which I soon found myself (this was in the winter of 1914), that Shershenevich, Bol'shakov and Mayakovsky were our enemies and that a dispute which was far from a joke was in progress with them. The prospect of a quarrel with a man who had once already astounded me and who had been attracting me from a distance more and more, surprised me not a whit. The whole originality of Novatorism consisted in this. The birth of "Centrifugue" was attended by endless rows the whole winter. The whole winter I knew nothing except that I was playing at party discipline, did nothing but sacrifice to it taste and conscience. I prepared myself again to give up whatever they wanted and whenever it was needed. But this time I overestimated my powers.

It was a hot day towards the end of May, and we were already seated in a teashop on the Arbat, when the three named above entered from the street noisily and youthfully, gave their hats to the waiter and without dropping their voices, which had just been drowned by the noise of trams and carthorses, made in our direction with an unconstrained dignity. They had beautiful voices. The subsequent tendency towards declamation in poetry sprang from them. They were dressed elegantly, we—untidily.

Our antagonists' position was from every point of view superior to our own.

While Bobrov sparred with Shershenevich—and the crux of the matter was that they had once picked a quarrel with us and we had replied even more rudely, and it was necessary to bring all this to an end—I watched Mayakovsky uninterruptedly. I think that was the first time I had observed him from near.

His "e" for "a," a piece of sheet-iron rocking his diction, was an actor's trait. His calculated hardness was easily interpretable as a distinguishing mark of other professions and conditions. He was not alone in his impressiveness. His friends sat beside him. Of them, one, like him, was playing the dandy, the other, like him, was an authentic poet. But all these similarities did not diminish Mayakovsky's exceptional quality but stressed it. As distinct from playing each game separately he played them all at once, in contempt of acting a part he played at life. The latter —without any thought one might have of his future end —one caught at a glance. And it was this which chained one to him and terrified one.

Although one can see at their full height anyone who is walking or standing up, the same circumstance on the appearance of Mayakovsky seemed miraculous, forcing everyone to turn in his direction. In his case the natural appeared supernatural. The reason for this was not his height, but another more general and less obvious peculiarity. To a greater extent than other people he was all in his appearance. He had as much of the expressive and final about him as the majority have little, issuing rarely as they do, and only in cases of exceptional upheavals, from the mists of unfathomable intentions and bankrupt conjectures. It was as if he existed on the day following a terrific spiritual life lived through for use in all

IV

We met by chance on the following day under the awning of the Greek café. The slice of large yellow boulevard stretched between Pushkin and Nikitin streets. Thin long-tongued dogs stretched, yawned and arranged their heads more comfortably on their front paws. Nannies, kindred souls, were talking scandal and lamenting about something or other. Butterflies suddenly folded their wings, melting in the heat, and as suddenly opened them, attracted sideways by the unequal waves of haze. A little girl in white, probably dripping, leapt in the air encircling herself from head to foot with the whistling rings of a skipping rope.

I saw Mayakovsky in the distance and pointed him out to Loks. He was playing at "heads or tails" with Khodasevich. At that moment Khodasevich got up, paid his losses and came out from the awning in the direction of Strastnoe. Mayakovsky was left alone at his table. We came in, greeted him and began talking. A little later he offered to read one or two things.

The poplars glimmered green. The limes glinted grey. The sleepy dogs driven out of all patience by the fleas leapt on all four paws at once and calling heaven to witness their moral helplessness against a brutal force flung themselves on the sand in a state of exasperated sleepiness. Engines on the Brestsk road, now changed to the Alexander, uttered hoarse whistles. And all around people cut hair, shaved, baked and fried, sold their wares, moved about—and saw nothing.

It was the tragedy *Vladimir Mayakovsky* which had just come out then. I listened raptly, with all my heart, holding my breath, forgetting all about myself. I had never heard anything like this before.

It contained everything. The boulevard, the dogs, the limes and the butterflies. The hairdressers, bakers, tailors and engines. Why cite them? We all remember the heat-oppressed mysterious summer text, now accessible to anyone in the tenth edition.

In the distance locomotives roared like the white sturgeon. In the hoarse cry of his creation lay the same absolute far distance as on earth. Here there was that profound animation, without which there is no originality, that infinity, which opens out from any one point of life in any direction, without which poetry is only a misunderstanding, something temporarily unexplained.

And how simple all this was! The creation was called a tragedy. And that is what it ought to be called. The tragedy was called "Vladimir Mayakovsky." The title contained the simple discovery of genius, that a poet is not an author, but—the subject of a lyric, facing the world in the first person. The title was not the name of the composer but the surname of the composition.

v

On that occasion I really carried him entire with me from the boulevard into my own life. But he was gigantic —it was impossible to retain him when apart. And I lost him. At that time he reminded me of himself. *The Cloud in Trousers, The Backbone Flute, War and Peace, Man.* The pieces which saw the light in the intervals were so tremendous that extraordinary reminders were needed. And such they were. Each of the stages named found me unprepared. At each stage, developing beyond recognition, he was born entirely anew, as for the first time. It was impossible to get used to him. What was it then that was so unusual about him?

When war was declared the weather broke, the rains
came and the first tears of the women streamed down.
The war was still new and terrifying in this newness. No
one knew how to treat it and it was like entering icy water.

The passenger trains in which the local people of the
district left for the mobilisation made their departures in
accordance with the old time-table. The train would start
and in its wake, beating its head on the rails, would roll a
wave of cuckoo-crying unlike weeping, unnaturally soft and
bitter like a rowanberry. An elderly woman wrapped up
unsuitably for summer would be swept off her feet and embraced. The relations of the recruit would draw her away
with monosyllabic persuasions beneath the station porch.

This lamentation which continued only for the first few
months, was wider than the grief of the young wives and
the mothers which was poured out into it. It was ushered
on to the line in perfect order. The station-masters
touched their caps as it passed them by, the telegraph poles
made way for it. It transformed the district, was everywhere visible in the pewter-cast of misfortune, because it
was an unaccustomed thing of burning brightness which
had lain untouched since wars gone by. They had taken it
from a secret place during the previous night and brought
it behind the horses to the station in the morning, and
after they had led it out by the hand from the station
porch they would carry it back along the bitter mud of the
village road. That was how they saw the men off who were
going as single volunteers or driving to town in green carriages with their fellow-countrymen.

But soldiers in ready marching order passing straight
into the horror itself were seen off without commotion.
With everything strapped on they jumped unpeasant-like
from the high railway trucks on to the sand, jingling their

spurs and trailing behind them through the air their over-coats which were thrown on anyhow. Others stood in the wagons at the cross-beams patting the horses, which stamped the dirty woodwork of the rotting floor with the proud beats of their hooves. The platform did not give away free apples, did not search its pocket for an answer, but flushing crimson laughed into the corners of tightly pinned kerchieves.

September was drawing to a close. Like a fire muddied with water a dusty gold nut tree burnt in the river vale, bent and broken by the winds and the climbers after nuts, an absurd image of desolation, doubled up at every joint in stubborn opposition to misfortune.

One day in August in the early afternoon the knives and plates on the terrace were tinged with green, twilight fell on the flower garden, the birds were hushed. The sky began to tear off the pale network of night with which it was deceptively overcast, as with an "invisible cap." The park, deathly still, gazed up in cross-eyed malevolence at the humiliating puzzle which was making something super-numerary of the earth in whose loud praise it had so proudly drunk with all its roots. A hedgehog rolled on to the path. A dead adder lay on it in an Egyptian hiero-glyphic which resembled a piece of string folded in a knot. The hedgehog moved it and suddenly dropped it and lay very still. And he broke and scattered his armful of needles again and stuck out and hid his snout. During the time the eclipse lasted, the ball of prickly suspicion con-tracted, now in a little boot, now in a lump, until the foreboding of a rising indecision drove it back to its hole.

VIII

In the winter, Z. M. M——, one of the S—— sisters took a flat in the Tversky Boulevard. People often dropped

like his subsequent somewhat more powerful attachment to L. Y. Brik which lasted till he died, was entirely natural. One did not suffer for Mayakovsky when he was in Bol'shakov's company, he was not divided against himself and did not demean himself.

Usually his sympathies aroused perplexity. A poet with an exhilaratingly great self-knowledge, who had gone further than any one else in stripping bare the lyrical element and in linking it to a giant theme with a medieval courage, until his poetry spoke with a voice which was almost that of sectarian identities, he seized on another more localised tradition with the same breath and strength.

He saw at his feet a city which gradually rose towards him from the depths of the Bronze Horseman, Crime and Punishment, Petersburg, a city covered with a haze which with unnecessary prolixity was called the problem of the Russian intellectuals, but which was in reality nothing more than a city covered with the haze of eternal conjectures about the future, the precarious Russian city of the nineteenth and twentieth centuries.

He embraced views such as these, and along with such immense contemplations he remained faithful, almost as though it were a duty, to the pygmy projects of his fortuitous coterie, hastily gathered together and always indecently mediocre. A man for whom truth held an almost animal attraction he surrounded himself with shallow dilettantes, men with fictitious reputations and false unwarranted pretensions. Or, what is more important: to the end he kept finding something in the veterans of a movement which he had himself abolished long ago and forever.

Probably these were the consequences of a fatal isolation, established and then voluntarily aggravated with that pedantry with which the will sometimes follows a road known to be inevitable.

But all this became intelligible only later. The symptoms of future singularities were then still very slight. Mayakovsky recited Akhmatova, Severyanin, his own and Bol'shakov's poems on the war and the city, and when we left our friends at night, the city lay deep in the rear of the firing line.

We were already failing to answer the problem which is always a difficult one in immense Russia—the problem of transport and supplies. Already out of new words: equipment, medicines, licences, refrigerators, the first grubs of speculation were being hatched. And while speculation thought in terms of transport, essential trainloads of fresh population were being conveyed hastily, day and night, to the sound of songs, in exchange for the casualties which returned in the hospital trains. And the best of the young girls and women became nurses.

The place for honest attitudes was the front, and the rear would have fallen into a false position anyway, even if it were not in addition voluntarily supporting a lie. Although no one was yet trying to catch it, the city hid behind phrases like a thief who has been apprehended. Like all hypocrites Moscow led an outwardly heightened existence and was brilliant with the artificial brilliance of a florist's window in winter.

At night the voice of Moscow seemed to resemble Mayakovsky's exactly. The events which took place there and the accumulating thunder of his voice were alike as two drops of water. But this was not that resemblance about which Naturalism dreams, but the connection which binds the anode to the cathode, the artist to life, the poet to his time.

The house of the head of the Moscow police stood

could not decide how. If I had been younger I would have abandoned literature. But my age was an obstacle. After all my metamorphoses I could not decide to alter course for the fourth time.

Something else happened. The times, and everything which influenced us both, bound me to Mayakovsky. We possessed certain things in common. I took note of them. I understood that unless one did something with oneself, these would become more numerous later: that he must be preserved from their triteness. Unable to define this I decided to renounce whatever it was which led me up to it. I abandoned the Romantic manner. And that is how the non-Romantic style of *Over the Barriers* came about.

But a whole conception of life lay concealed under the Romantic manner which I was to deny myself from henceforth. This was the conception of life as the life of the poet. It had come down to us from the Symbolists and had been adapted by them from the Romantics, principally the Germans.

This conception had influenced Blok but only during a short period. It was incapable of satisfying him in the form in which it came naturally to him. He could either heighten it or abandon it altogether. He abandoned the conception. Mayakovsky and Esenin heightened it.

In the poet who imagines himself the measure of life and pays for this with his life, the Romantic conception manifests itself brilliantly and irrefutably in his symbolism, that is in everything which touches upon Orphism and Christianity imaginatively. In this sense something inscrutable was incarnate both in the life of Mayakovsky and in the fate of Esenin, which defies all epithets, demanding self-destruction and passing into myth.

But outside the legend, the Romantic scheme is false. The poet who is its foundation, is inconceivable without the non-poets who must bring him into relief, because this poet is not a living personality absorbed in the study of moral knowledge, but a visual-biographical "emblem," demanding a background to make his contours visible. In contradistinction to the Passion Plays which needed a Heaven if they were to be heard, this drama needs the evil of mediocrity in order to be seen, just as Romanticism always needs philistinism and with the disappearance of the petty bourgeoisie loses half its poetical content.

A scenic conception of biography was inherent in my time. I shared this conception with everyone else. I abandoned it before it had yet hardened into a duty with the Symbolists, before it bore any implication of heroism and before it smelt of blood. And in the first place, I freed myself from it unconsciously, abandoning the Romantic method for which it served as basis. In the second place, I shunned it consciously also, considering its brilliance unsuited to my craft and feared any kind of poetising which would place me in a false and incongruous position.

When *My Sister, Life* appeared, and was found to contain expressions not in the least contemporary as regards poetry, which were revealed to me during the summer of the revolution, I became entirely indifferent as to the identity of the power which had brought the book into being because it was immeasurably greater than myself and than the poetical conceptions surrounding me.

XII

From the Sivtsev-Vrazhek the winter twilight, the roofs and trees of the Arbat gazed into a dining-room which was not turned out for whole months at a time. The owner of the flat, a bearded journalist of extraordinary absent-mindedness and good nature, produced the impression of being a bachelor, although he possessed a family in the

attention. One divined in her that readiness which is dear to me, the readiness to part with any habits and privileges when something great kindles one's passion and arouses admiration. On that occasion we exchanged a few candid, friendly words. At that evening gathering she was for me a palladium against the representatives of the two movements, Futurist and Symbolist, who thronged the room.

The reading began. They read by seniority without any perceptible success. When it came to Mayakovsky's turn, he got up and clasping the edge of an empty shelf which overhung the back of the divan, he began to read *Man*. Like a bas-relief, with time his background, as I always imagined him, he towered above those who were seated and those who were standing, and, now supporting his fine head with his hand, now resting his knee on the bolster of the divan, he read this poem with its unusual depth and its exalted inspiration.

Andrei Biely was sitting opposite him with Margarita Sabashnikov. He had lived in Switzerland during the war. The revolution brought him back to his own country. And probably, he was seeing and hearing Mayakovsky for the first time. He listened as one entranced and although he made no show of enthusiasm, his face spoke the more eloquently for that. He gazed at the man reading in amazement and gratitude. I could not see all the people listening, Tsvetaeva and Ehrenburg among them. I observed those I could see. The majority never abandoned the jealous self-respect which framed them. They all felt that they were names, that they were all—poets. Only Biely listened, entirely lost within himself, carried away by a joy which regrets nothing, because on the heights where it feels itself at home, only sacrifices exist and the eternal eagerness for these.

Chance brought together before my eyes the two

geniuses who justified the two literary tendencies which exhausted themselves one after another. Close to Biely whose proximity I experienced with a proud joy, I felt the presence of Mayakovsky with a redoubled strength. He was revealed to me with all the freshness of a first encounter. That evening I experienced this for the last time.

Many years went by after this. One year later he was the first to whom I read *My Sister, Life,* and I heard ten times more from him than I ever expected to hear from anyone. Another year passed. He read "150,000,000" to his own intimate circle. And for the first time I had nothing to say to him. Many years went by. We met in Russia and abroad, we tried to continue our intimacy, we tried to work together and I found myself understanding him less and less. Others will tell of this period, for during these years I came up against the limits of my understanding, and these, so it seems, were not to be enlarged. Reminiscences of this period would be colourless and would add nothing further to what I have said. Therefore I shall go straight on to what there remains for me to tell.

XIV

I shall tell of that eternally recurring strangeness which may be called the poet's last year.

Suddenly the projects which have not been realised come to an end. Often nothing is added to their lack of realisation except the new and only now admissable certainty that they have been realised. And this certainty is handed down to posterity.

Men change their habits, busy themselves with new plans, never cease to boast of their spiritual uplift. And suddenly—the end, sometimes violent, often natural, but even then, because there is no desire to defend oneself,

It sticks out in the backs of fur coats and sledges; like a silver coin it rolls on its rim over the ground along the rails, far into the distance, where it gently tumbles flat in the mist and is picked up by a signalman's wife in a sheepskin jacket. It spins, grows small, seethes with contingencies. It is so easy to stumble on a slight want of attention in it! These are unpleasantnesses deliberately imagined. They are fanned up consciously out of nothing. But even when they have been blown upon they remain completely insignificant beside the wrongs which were so triumphantly trampled upon a short while ago. And that's the whole point, this latter defies comparison because it happened in that previous existence, which it was such a joy to tear asunder. Oh, if only this joy were more equable and more plausible!

But it is incredible and incomparable, and yet this joy hurls one from extreme to extreme as nothing else in life can ever hurl one anywhere.

And how discouraged people get at this! How Andersen with his hapless duckling repeats himself! What mountains are made out of molehills!

But perhaps the inner voice lies? Perhaps the terrible world is right?

"No smoking," "State your business briefly!" Are these not truths?

"He? Hang himself? Don't you worry."

"In love?——He?——Ha—ha—ha! He loves himself alone."

A large, a real and a realistically existing city. Winter and frost. In twenty degrees of frost, as if on stakes that have been driven into the ground, the creaking willow-plaited atmosphere hangs athwart the road. Everything there grows misty, rolls away and is hidden. But can there be such sadness when there is such joy? Is this not the second birth then? Is this death?

XV

In the registry offices for the births, deaths and marriages of citizens, there are no instruments for measuring truth; sincerity is not measured by X rays. Nothing besides firmness in the stranger's hand as he makes the entry, is necessary to make the registration valid. And after that no doubts are raised and the matter is not discussed further.

He will write his last letter in his own hand, bequeathing his treasure to the world as something obvious; he will measure his own sincerity and illumine it with an unalterable end; and now they will begin to discuss it, to doubt, to make comparisons.

They compare her with his previous loves, but she resembles him alone and all that precedes him. They make conjectures about his sentiment and do not know that one can love, not only for a day, even if it is forever, but also even if it is not forever, for the perfect accumulation of past days.

But two expressions have long reached a common triviality: a genius and a beautiful woman. And how much they have in common.

Her movements have been constrained since childhood. She is beautiful and she found this out early in life. And the so-called world of nature is the one place where she can be herself to the full, because when with others it is impossible to take a step without hurting others or herself being hurt.

A young girl, she leaves the house. What does she think of doing? She has already been receiving letters at the poste-restante. She has let two or three friends into her secret. Let us admit all this: she is going to a rendez-vous.

She leaves the house. She would like the night to notice her, the heart of the air to be wrung at the sight of her, the stars to find something to say of her. She would like to

dren loudly proclaimed their presence abroad. In the early spring their voices are strangely far-reaching, in spite of the busy roar of the town.

The tram clambered slowly up the Svivaya slope. There is a place there where first the pavement on the right and then the pavement on the left approach so close to the windows of the tram, that when you hold on to the strap you make an involuntary bending movement over Moscow, as over an old woman who has slipped, for she suddenly falls on all fours and divests herself dully of her watch-makers and shoe-makers, lifts and rearranges roofs of some sort and belfries, then all of a sudden stands up, shaking the hem of her skirt, and drives the tram down a level and uninteresting street.

This time the movements of the town were so clearly an extract from the dead man's life, that is, they reminded one so powerfully of something significant in his being, that I shivered all over, and the famous telephone call from *The Cloud* thundered through me of its own accord, as if it was being uttered loudly by someone at my side. I was standing on the platform next to S—— and bent towards her to remind her of the eight lines but . . . "I feel that my 'I' is too small for me" . . . made my lips cling together like fingers in mittens, and I was so moved that I could not say a word.

Two empty motor cars were standing at the end of the Hendrikov mews. They were surrounded by an inquisitive crowd.

In the hall and in the dining-room men with and without hats were either sitting or standing. He was lying farther off, in his own study. The door from the hall into Lilya's room was open, and on the threshold, with his hand pressed against the lintel, Aseyev was crying. In the depths of the room by the window, his head sunk between his shoulders, Kirsanov was shaking with silent sobs.

The sodden mist of mourning was interspersed even here with anxious conversation carried on in a low voice, as at the end of a requiem, when after a service as sticky as jam, the first whispered words are so dry that they seem to come from under the floorboards and to smell of mice. In one of these intervals the porter carefully entered the room, a chisel inserted into his top-boot, and he removed the winter frame and opened the windows slowly and noiselessly. It was still cold outside without a coat, and sparrows and children were encouraging one another with their aimless chirping.

Leaving the dead man on tiptoe someone asked softly whether a telegram had been sent off to Lilya. L. A. G. replied that it had been sent. Zhenia took me aside and drew my attention to the courage with which L. A. was bearing the terrible burden of the catastrophe. She began to cry. I squeezed her hand firmly.

The apparent indifference of the boundless world poured in through the window. Along its whole length, grey trees stood guarding a frontier which seemed to divide earth and sea. I gazed at the branches with their warm, eager buds and tried to imagine that scarcely conceivable London, far, far, beyond the trees, where the telegram had gone. Soon, over there, someone would cry out, stretch her hands towards us, fall down unconscious. My throat was constricted. I decided to enter his room once more and weep my fill.

He lay on his side, his face turned towards the wall, sombre, tall, a sheet covering him to his chin, his mouth half open as in sleep. Turning proudly away from us all, even when he was lying down, even in this sleep, he was going away from us in a stubborn endeavour to reach something. His face recalled the time, when he had spoken of himself as "beautiful in his twenty-two years," [11] for death had ossified a mask which rarely falls into its clutches.

Suddenly there was a movement in the hall. Alone, apart from her mother and sister, who were already giving way to their grief inaudibly in the crowd, the younger sister of the dead man, Ol'ga Vladimirovna, entered the flat. She entered possessively and noisily. Her voice floated into the room before her. Mounting the stairs alone she was speaking to someone in a loud voice, addressing her brother openly. Then she herself came into view, and walking through the crowd as through a rubbish pit, she reached her brother's door, threw up her hands and stood still. "Volodya!" she screamed in a voice which echoed through the whole house. A second flashed by. "He says nothing! He doesn't answer. Volodya. Volodya! How terrible!"

She was falling. They caught her up and quickly began to restore her to consciousness. She had hardly come to herself, when she moved greedily towards the body and sitting down at his feet, precipitately resumed her unexhausted dialogue. At last, as I had long desired, I burst into tears.

It had been impossible to cry like this in the place where he had killed himself, for there the gregarious spirit of drama had swiftly crowded out the explosive vividness of fact. Over there the asphalt courtyard stank of the deification of the inevitable as of saltpetre, that is, it stank of the false fatalism of towns, which has arisen from a simian mimicry and conceives life as a chain of sensations capable of faithful reproduction. There had been weeping over there too, but only because the constricted throat could

[11] A reference to a phrase in the first part of Mayakovsky's *Cloud in Trousers*, written at the age of twenty-two.—*Translator's Note*.

reproduce with its animal second-sight the convulsions of inhabited houses, fire-escapes, a revolver case, of all those things which make one sick with despair and vomit with murder.

His sister was the first to mourn for him in her own way and as she wished to do, to mourn as people mourn for something great, and to the accompaniment of her words one could cry boundlessly and insatiably, as to the giant lament of an organ.

She would not be checked. "The bath-house for them!" [12]—Mayakovsky's own voice cried out indignantly, strangely transmuted by his sister's contralto. "To make it more amusing. They laughed. They called for him—And this is what was happening to him. Why didn't you come to us, Volodya?" she moaned through her sobs, but controlling herself, she moved closer to him impulsively. "Do you remember, do you remember, Volodichka?" she suddenly reminded him almost as though he were still alive, and began to recite:

"I feel that my 'I' is too small for me.
Someone is obstinately breaking out of me.
Hullo!
Who's there? Mother?

Mother! Your son is marvellously ill.
Mother! His heart is on fire.
Tell his sisters Lyudya and Olya,
He has nowhere to go." [13]

[12] An allusion to Mayakovsky's satirical play The Bath-house. —Translator's Note.

[13] This is a literal rendering, doing no justice to the poetry.— Translator's Note.

When I returned in the evening, he was already in his coffin. The faces which had filled the room during the day had given place to others. It was comparatively quiet. There was scarcely any more weeping.

Suddenly, outside, underneath the window I imagined I saw his life, which now already belonged entirely to the past. I saw it move away obliquely from the window like a quiet tree-bordered street resembling the Povarskaya. And the first to take its stand in this street, by the very wall, was our State, our unprecedented and unbelievable State, rushing headlong towards the ages and accepted by them for ever. It stood there below, one could hail it and take it by the hand. Its palpable strangeness somehow recalled the dead man. The resemblance was so striking that they might have been twins.

And it occurred to me then in the same irrelevant way that this man was perhaps this State's unique citizen. The novelty of the age flowed climatically through his blood. His strangeness was the strangeness of our times of which half is as yet to be fulfilled. I began to recall traits in his character, his independence, which in many ways, was completely original. All these were explained by his familiarity with states of mind which though inherent in our time, have not yet reached full maturity. He was spoilt from childhood by the future, which he mastered rather early and apparently without great difficulty.

(1931)

Translated by Beatrice Scott

AERIAL WAYS

I

THE NURSE was sleeping under the age-old mulberry tree, leaning against its trunk. When the enormous lilac-coloured cloud appeared at the end of the road, silencing the grasshoppers which were chirping sultrily in the long grass, and while the drums in the camp sighed and died away, the earth grew dark, and there was no life in the world.

"Where, oh where," came the continual cry from the hare-lip of the half-witted shepherdess; and preceded by a steer, dragging one of her legs, brandishing a wild twig as though it was lightning, she came out of dust-laden cloud at the end of the garden, where the thickets began: deadly nightshade, bricks, twisted wire and evil-smelling shadows.

She disappeared. The cloud threw a glance at the baked and undistinguished stubble earth which lay scattered over the horizon. Gently the cloud reared upwards. The stubble earth extended far away, beyond the camp. The cloud fell on its forelegs, and smoothly crossing the road, noiselessly crawled along the fourth railway line of the shunting. The bushes uncovered their heads and moved with the whole bank behind them. They flowed backwards, greeting the cloud. She did not answer them.

Berries and caterpillars fell from the trees. They fell, tainted with heat, poured down on the nurse's apron and ceased to think of anything.

The child was crawling towards the conduit. Already he had been crawling for a long time. Now he started to climb farther up.

And when the rain comes, and when both pairs of railway tracks fly along the bending wattles, preserving themselves from the black and liquid night which will fall upon them, and when this liquid night, raging, hurriedly cries to you not to be afraid, telling you that her name is shower or love or something else, I shall tell you of the parents of the ravished child who have cleaned their white linen dresses early in the evening, and of how it was still very early when, dressed in snow-white as for tennis, they walked through the still shadows of the garden and reached the post on which they could read the name of the station, and at that moment the swollen plates of the steam-engine rolled over the garden and enveloped the Turkish cake-shop in clouds of short-winded yellow smoke.

They walked to the harbour to meet the midshipman who once loved her, who remained a friend of her husband, and who was expected this morning in the town after achieving his master's certificate.

The husband was burning with impatience to initiate his friend into the deep significance of fatherhood, which had not yet become tiresome to him. So it often happens. Something quite simple brings you, perhaps for the first time, to the gates of something substantial and significant. It is so new to you that when you meet a man who has gone round the world and seen much and has much to tell, it suddenly occurs to you that in any conversation he will be the listener, while the loquacious one is you, astonishing him with your eloquence.

In contrast to her husband it dragged her, like an anchor in water, into the iron clamour of the harbor, towards the red rust of the three-funnelled giants, towards the grain flowing in rivers, under the luminous splash of sky, of ships' sails and sailors. But their motives were not the same.

The rain falls, falls as from a pail: I must begin the work I have promised myself. The branches of a hazel-nut tree crackle over a ditch. Two figures run across a field. The man wears a black beard. The woman's dishevelled hair blows in the wind. The man wears a green kaftan and silver ear-rings. In his hands he holds the delighted child. The rain falls, as from a pail.

II

It occurred to him that he had been promoted midshipman a long time ago. Eleven o'clock at night. The last train from the town rolled to the station. Having cried to its heart's content, it became agitated after making the turn, and began to flurry. Now, drawing into its bursting reservoir all the surrounding air, the leaves, the sand, the dew, it stood still, clapped its hands and became silent, awaiting the answering roar. The echo should have flown into him along all the pathways. And when it heard it, a woman, a sailor and a civilian in white would turn away from the big road towards the footpath, and right in front of them, from under the poplars, there would arise the brilliant surface of the dewy roof. They would walk to the hedge, losing sight of none of the grooves, bolts and cornices which hung on it like ear-rings; while the iron planet begins to sink away as they draw near. The rumble of the disappearing train would grow unexpectedly huge and deceive itself and others for a short time with a feigned silence, and disperse later in a thin rain of soapsuds which disappear in the distance.

But it would then appear that it was not the train at all,

but only rockets of water with which the sea was amusing itself. The moon would move behind the station trees on the edge of the road. Then, looking at the landscape, you would realize that it was invented by a well-known poet, whose name you have forgotten, and they would give it to children at Christmas. You would remember too that this enclosure once appeared in your dreams, where it was known as "the end of the world."

A pail of paint shines white against the porch, washed with the light of the moon, the paintbrush standing against the wall with the tip pointed upwards. They opened a window into the garden. "To-day they are painting the house white"—from the lips of a soft-voiced woman. "Can you feel it? Now come and have supper." Once more the silence settled down on them. It lasted only a short time. Confusion entered the house. "What do you mean— not there? Disappeared?" cries a hoarse bass voice which resembles the voice of a relaxed violin string, and at the same time the hysterical gathering contralto of a woman's voice. "Under the tree? Under the tree? Stand up immediately. And don't howl! For Christ's sake let go my hands. My God!—it is not possible. My Tosha! My Toshenka! Don't dare, don't dare to say it. What a shameless woman you are, you good-for-nothing, you shameless—" An end to words, voices mournfully meeting, pausing, moving into the distance. It was no longer possible to hear them.

Night came to an end, but the dawn was still far away. The earth lay covered with shadows, like hayricks, stupefied by silence. The shadows were at rest. The distances between them increased, compared with distances during the day, as though they could lie down better: the shadows scattered and moved into the distance. In the intervals between them the ice-cold meadows puffed silently and

136

sniffed under their sweating horse-cloths. Sometimes these shadows assumed the shape of a tree or a cloud or something recognisable. The majority were vague, nameless piles. They were not quite sure of their surroundings, and in the half-darkness it was almost impossible to tell whether the rain had ceased or whether it was gathering and beginning to fall in drops. They were thrown incessantly from the past into the future, from the future into the past, like sand in an hour-glass repeatedly turned over.

And on a distant level from theirs, like linen plucked at dawn by a gust of wind from the fence-walls and carried heaven knows where, three human figures gleamed confusedly on the edge of the field. On the side opposite them the eternally evaporating roar of the distant sea rumbled towards them. These four things were borne from the past into the future; but not in the contrary direction. People in white were running from place to place, they bent down, straightened out, jumped into ditches, disappeared and then reappeared alongside the trench at some altogether different place. Finding themselves at a great distance from one another, they shouted and waved their hands, and since their signals were frequently misunderstood, some of them began to wave more violently, more vexatiously and more often, making signs that they did not understand the signals, that they should be cancelled out, that they should not turn back but continue looking where they were looking before. The harmony and violence of their figures made an impression reminding one of football played at night— they had lost the ball and were searching for it in the ditch, and when they found it they would continue the game.

Among the supine shapes calm reigned supreme, and one could even believe in the approaching dawn, but at the sight of these people flying up like a whirlwind over the land, it occurred to you that the valley was buffeted

137

and whipped into motion by the wind, darkness and fear, as though by a black comb with three broken teeth.

There exists a law according to which nothing, which is continually happening to others, happens to us. This is a law which is not infrequently referred to by authors. The irrefutability of this doctrine is proved by the fact that as long as our friends recognise us, we believe that the mischief can be cured. When we are completely convinced that it is incurable, our friends cease to recognise us; and as though to confirm the law, we ourselves became quite different, we became those whose vocation it is to be consumed, to be ruined, to be put on trial or in a lunatic asylum. While they were yet healthy people, they vented their anger on the nurse; and somehow they thought that it depended wholly upon the impetuousness of their justice whether they would go to the child's bedroom and there, with a sigh of relief find the child restored to its place by the greatness of their fear and anxiety. The sight of the empty bed deprived them of their voices. But even when their souls were wounded, even while they were throwing themselves in a fervid search round the garden, and still continuing their search, moved further and further away from the house: even when they were in this state of mind, they remained for a long time men *like others*, that is, they were searching in order to find. Time changed. The night changed its face and they too changed. Now, towards the end of the night, they were quite unrecognisable; they were people who had ceased to understand the meaning of life, and they gave themselves no time to take breath, while the violence of space harried them from one end of the land to the other, the land on which they would never again see their son. And they had forgotten the midshipman who was continuing his search on the other side of the ravine.

Is it on the strength of this doubtful observation that

the author conceals things which are well-known to him from the reader? He knows indeed better than any other that as soon as they open the baker's shop in the village and as soon as the first trains begin to speed through, the rumour of disaster will flow from house to house, and finally show the two pupils of the gymnasium from Olgina where they are to bring their nameless acquaintance the trophy of yesterday's victory.

Already from under the trees, as from under a hood pulled deeply over the eyes, came the beginning of unrevealed morning light. The day dawned in sudden storms, interruptedly. The roar of the sea instantly disappeared, and everything became still more silent than before. Coming from no one knows where, a sweet insistent tremor passed through the trees. One by one, and one after another, having touched the wattles with a silver perspiration, the trees, which were agitated a moment before, fell asleep. Two rare diamonds flashed intermittently and independently in the deep nest of this shadowy blessedness: a bird and a bird's twittering. Afraid of solitude, ashamed of its insignificance, the bird attempted to dissolve itself completely, with all its strength, in the vast sea of dew: unable to collect its thoughts in dream or sleep. It succeeded. It inclined its head to one side, firmly closed its eyes and without a sound surrendered itself to the stupidity and melancholy of the new-born earth; and took delight in the surrender. But the effort was finally too great for its strength. Suddenly breaking through its reserve and completely betraying itself, the powerful chirping sparkled like a cold star, an immutable pattern projected upon the immutability of space, the resilient voice flying away in thorn-shaped specks of light, echoes and jets of sound which grew cold and surprised, as though one had spilled a saucer with a vast astonished eye.

Then it grew light more quickly. The whole garden became filled with moist, white light. This light clung most strongly to the stucco wall, to the paths strewn with gravel and the trunks of fruit trees, which were covered with a kind of vitriolic, whitish composition like lime. And now, with a similar cold patina on her face, the child's mother, returning from the field, traced her plaited path through the garden. Without pausing, she walked full-tilt towards the back of the garden, without seeing the ground she was treading on, or what her feet were sinking in. The rise and fall of the waves of vegetables along the borders threw her backwards and forwards, as though her emotions were still in need of agitation. Crossing the kitchen-garden, she approached that part of the fence from which she could see the road leading to the camp. Here came the midshipman, who had decided to climb the fence instead of making a detour round the garden. The yawning east bore him towards the fence like the white sail of a violently tilted boat. She waited for him, clinging to the garden rails. Obviously she had decided to say something and had already prepared a short speech.

The same proximity of the rain in the sky, fallen recently or merely expected, could be felt on the seashore. Where did the roar come from, which could be heard all night on the other side of the railway track? The sea lay still, freezing, like the quick-silver coating of a mirror, and only in the sands it changed its mind and whimpered. The horizon was becoming yellow, diseased, an evil ochreous colour. Certainly this dawn deserved an excuse, this dawn which was pressing close to the backwall of the vast, soiled, hundred-verst-long stable, where at any moment and from any direction waves might rage and rear their heads. Meanwhile they were crawling on their stomachs, chafing one another, like a herd of innumerable black and

140

slippery pigs. From the rock on the shore descended the midshipman. He moved with quick, sprightly steps, often jumping from stone to stone. At the garden wall he had learned something which stupefied him. From the sand he picked up a piece of black tile and threw it skimming over the water. The stone, as though slipping over spittle, ricochetted sideways, uttering the same elusive childlike sound as the shoal-water surrounding it. Just at the moment when, losing all hope of finding the child, he turned towards the house and walked towards it along the edge of the clearing, Lelia ran out of the house, leaned over the fence, told him to come closer and said quickly: "We can't bear it any longer. Save us. Find him. He is your son." As soon as he had seized her hand, she broke away and ran off, and when he climbed into the garden, he found her nowhere. Once more he picked up a stone; and without ceasing to throw stones, he began to withdraw and he disappeared behind a projection in the rock. His own footprints stirred and quivered behind him. They too wanted to sleep. The gravel, disturbed in its calm, crept forward, fell away, sighed and turned from side to side; it tried to lie down as comfortably as possible in order to sleep at last in perfect peace.

III

More than fifteen years passed. The light grew dark in the courtyard, the rooms lay in shadow. Three times had the unknown woman asked to see the member of the presidium of the provincial executive council, the former naval officer Polivanov. In front of the woman stood a bored soldier. Through the lobby window could be seen a yard littered with brick-piles covered in snow. At the end, where once there had been a cesspool, there stood a pile of rubbish which had certainly not been thrown there recently. There the sky was like a wild grove, growing along the slopes of this accumulation of dead cats and potted-meat tins, which rose from the dead when it thawed and taking breath, began to smell of all the springs of the past, and of dripping, twittering, rattling freedom. But it was enough simply to turn away from this corner of the court-yard and gaze at the sky to be amazed by its newness.

The sky's present aptitude for spreading the sound of gunfire and rifle-fire coming from the sea and the railway station—and doing this for whole days—removed it a long way from its memories of 1905. Metalled, as by a steam-roller, from one end to the other by the everlasting cannonade and now finally rammed down and slain by it, it knit its brows and without showing any signs of movement moved away elsewhere, like a railway track monotonously unwinding its ribbon in winter.

What sort of sky was it? Even during the day it suggested the shape of nights during our youths, or during a journey. Even during the day it caught the eyes, immeasurable, noticeable. Even during the day it was saturated with the desolation of earth, and it struck down the somnolent and raised the dreamers to their feet.

There were aerial ways. And on them every day, like a train, came the rectilinear thoughts of a Liebknecht, a Lenin, a few other minds of the same greatness. They were paths set on a level, able and powerful enough to cross any frontier, whatever its name. One of these lines, opened during the war, preserved its former strategical height and owing to the nature of the frontiers through which they traced it, obtruded themselves upon the builders of these frontiers. This ancient military line, intersecting the frontiers of Poland and later of Germany on its own plane and in its own time—here, at the very beginning, manifestly

142

escaped from the understanding mediocrity and the endurance of mediocrity. It passed above the courtyard, which remained shy of the far-sightedness of its destination and its oppressive size, just as a suburb runs helter-skelter away from the railways and fears them. This was the sky of the Third International.

The soldier replied to the woman and said that Polivanov had not yet returned. Three different kinds of tedium could be heard in his voice. The tedium of a life lived in continual contact with liquid mud and of finding himself surrounded by dry dust. The tedium of a man who has accustomed himself in raiding and requisitioning parties to asking questions which ladies of this kind have to answer, confused and cowering, and also bored, because the sequence of orderly conversation was reversed and destroyed. Finally, it was the assumed indifference with which people allowed even the most extraordinary things to be normal. Knowing perfectly that the recent order must seem unbearable to the lady, he feigned stupid obstinacy, as though incapable of guessing her feelings, and as though he had never breathed an air other than that of dictatorship.

Suddenly Levushka entered. Something like the cable of a Giant's Stride threw him on to the second floor from the open air, whence came gusts of snow and unilluminated silence. Catching hold of this mysterious "something" which happened to be a portfolio, the soldier stopped the man from coming in, exactly as you might stop a merry-go-round. "What is the matter?" He turned to the man. There were delegates from the war-prisoners here. "Is it because of the Hungarians?" "Yes." "But they have already been told that they can't sail on the strength of documents alone." "That's what I said." "It all depends on the ships, I understand it all perfectly. I explained it to them in exactly the same terms." "And what then?" "They said,

'They knew all about it without my help. My job is to put the papers in order, as for an embarkation. And then, so to say, everything would go on swimmingly. And that we should give them a house.'" "Good, and what else?" "Nothing else, only the papers and the house." "No!" Polivanov interrupted him. "Why repeat it all over again? I am not talking about that." "A parcel from the Kanatnaya," said the soldier, mentioning the street where the Cheka presided; and as he approached Polivanov, he lowered his voice to a whisper, as though he were on parade. "What are you talking about? Aha! Impossible," Polivanov said absentmindedly, and with an air of complete indifference. The soldier moved away from him. For a moment both remained silent. "Have you brought the bread?" the soldier asked with unexpected bitterness, because the shape of the portfolio made the question unnecessary and he continued: "And then there is . . . There is a woman waiting for you . . ." "Of course," Polivanov drawled, with the same air of indifference. The cable of the Giant's Stride quivered and drew tight. The portfolio began to move. "Please, comrade," he turned to the woman and invited her into the study. He did not recognise her.

In comparison with the darkness of the hall, there was here complete obscurity. She followed him and stood still behind the doors. Probably there was a carpet laid over the whole room because after he made one or two steps, he disappeared and soon afterwards the sound of his footsteps could be heard at the opposite end of the darkness. Then sounds were heard, and gradually the table became furnished with glasses which were being removed, with the remains of sugar and toast, with the parts of a disjointed revolver, with hexagonal pencils. He was quietly fingering the table, sliding his hands quickly over its surface and searching for matches. Her imagination had hardly time to situate the room, hung with pictures and littered with cupboards, palms and a bronze in one of the avenues of pre-revolutionary Petersburg, when it suddenly appeared with a cluster of lights in its outstretched hand ready to illuminate all the perspectives; and suddenly the telephone bell rang. This gurgling sound, recalling a field or the outskirts of a town, immediately reminded her that the wire had found its way through a town plunged in complete darkness, and all this was happening in the province under the rule of the Bolsheviks.

"Yes"—answered the man, dissatisfied, impatient, mortally tired. (Probably he was covering his eyes with his hands.) "Yes. I know. I know. Nonsense. You should verify it. Nonsense. I was connected with the staff. Zhmerinka replied a whole hour ago. Is that all? Yes, of course I will. I shall talk to them. No. In twenty minutes, then. Is that all?"

"Well, comrade." He turned to the woman who was his guest, with a box in one hand and a drop of sulphureous blue flame in the other; and then, almost at the moment when the matches dropped and scattered on the floor, there came the rising sound of her perturbed but distinct whisper.

"Lelia!" Polivanov shouted out of his mind. "It can't be —I'm sorry—not really—Lelia!"

"Yes, yes. Let me calm myself. Strange that we should meet," Lelia whispered, monotonously choking back her tears.

Suddenly everything vanished. By the light of a glimmering oil-lamp they faced one another, the man in a short unbuttoned jacket, corroded from too little sleep, and the woman who came from the station and had not washed for a long time. As though youth and the sea had never

145

been. In the light of the oil-lamp her journey, the death of Dmitri and of the daughter of whose existence he knew nothing and, in short, all that had been told to him before the lamp was lit, appeared depressing in the necessary truth which was inviting the listener to the grave, unless his sympathies were indeed no more than vain words. Regarding her in the light of the lamp, he at once remembered why they had not kissed when they first met. Smiling involuntarily, he wondered at the tenacity of prejudice. In the light of the oil-lamp all her hopes about the decoration of the room vanished. As to the man, he appeared so strange that it was impossible to ascribe this sensation of strangeness to any change in the light. So she returned to the subject of her own affairs all the more decisively, and as she had done once before, she began to tell her story blindly and by heart, as though relating a message which was strange to her.

"If you have any love for your child—" she began. "Again—" Polivanov momentarily flared up and began to speak, to speak, to speak—quickly and without pause. He spoke as he would write an article, with who's and with commas. He paced up and down the room, he paused from time to time, he waved his hands and made gestures. In the intervals he wrinkled the skin over his nose and plucking the folds with his fingers, he rubbed and irritated the place, as if it were the source of an exhausting and burning indignation. He begged her to stop thinking that people were more debased than she imagined, to stop thinking that one could ill-treat them as one liked. He invoked her by all that was sacred not to pursue this nonsensical diatribe, especially since she had herself confessed to fraud. He said that even if all this rigamarole were accepted as the truth, she would achieve an entirely different aim from the one she was looking forward to. It is impossible to explain to a man that something which did not exist a moment before and now suddenly appeared in his life was not a discovery but a complete loss. He remembered the lightheartedness and freedom which he felt when he believed her story, and how he had no desire at all to ransack any more ditches and canals, and wanted only to bathe in the sea. "So that, even if time flowed backwards—" he tried to taunt her, and again he would have to search one of the members of her family, and then too he would be disturbing himself only for her sake and for the sake of X and Y, but not for his own sake or for her ridiculous . . . "Have you finished?" she asked, leaving him to exhaust his anger. "You're quite right. I took back all I said. Don't you understand? Perhaps it was mean and cowardly. I was mad with joy because the boy was found. And how marvellous it was. Do you remember? I hadn't the courage to break my life and the life of Dmitri. I renounced myself. Now my fate has no importance. He is yours. Leva, Leva, if only you knew in what danger he is now. I don't know how to begin. Take things in their proper order. From that day we haven't seen one another. You don't know him. He's so trustful. Some day his trust will ruin him. There is a scamp, an adventurer—God be his judge. Neploshaiev, Tosha's school-friend."

Hearing these words Polivanov stopped walking about the room and stood as though rooted to the ground. He ceased to hear her. She mentioned a name which had been mentioned among many others some minutes ago by the whispering soldier. He knew this case. The position was hopeless for the accused, and all would be over in an hour. "Did he act under his real name?" She grew pale when she heard this question. It meant that he knew more than she knew, and the situation was even worse than she thought. She forgot in which camp he was, and imagining

147

that his sin lay only in the fictitious name, she began to justify his son in a false direction. "But, Leva, he could not openly defend . . ." And again he ceased to hear her, he understood that her child might be concealed in any of the names he knew from the documents, and he stood by the table and rang someone up and he tried to get some news and from one argument to another he moved further and deeper into the town and the night, until the abyss of the last and ultimate truth lay revealed before him.

He looked round the room. Lelia had vanished. He felt as though he had received a terrible blow between the eyes, and when he looked round the room, it swam before him like stalactites, like rivers. He wanted to pluck the skin over the bridge of his nose, and instead he put his hand to his eyes and in doing this, the stalactites began to dance and disappear. It would have been easier for him if their convulsions had been less frequent, and not so silent. At last he found her. Like a large, unbruised doll she was lying between the table and the chair, in the very same layer of rubbish and dust which in the darkness and when she had not yet lost consciousness, she had taken for a carpet.

(1924)

Translated by Robert Payne

LETTERS FROM TULA

I

In the air the larks were pouring out their song, and in the train coming from Moscow the suffocating sun was borne on innumerable striped divans. The sun sank. A bridge with the inscription UPA swam past a hundred windows at the same moment that the fireman, flying ahead of the train, in the tender, discovered in the roar of his own hair and the cool excitement of evening on the side away from the track, the town which was speedily being carried towards them.

And meanwhile, over there, greeting one another in the streets, they said: "Good evening." Some added: "Have you come from there?" "No, we're going there," others answered. One objected: "It's late. It's all over."

"Tula, the 10th.

So now you have changed into another compartment, as arranged with the conductor. A moment ago the general who offered you his seat, came to the buffet and bowed to me as to an old acquaintance. The next train for Moscow leaves at three o'clock at night. The general said good-bye as he went away. The porter opens the door for him. The *izvozchiks* are clamouring. In the distance they seemed to be twittering like sparrows. Darling, this farewell was so senseless. Now our separation is ten times more unbearable. From this point my imagination begins. It rankles in me. The horse tramway is coming from over there, they are changing the horses. I shall go and have a look at the town.

O nostalgia! I shall beat her, blunt her, my furious nostalgia, with verses."

.   .   .   .   .

"Tula.

Alas, there is no middle way. One must go at the second bell or follow a common path to the end, to the grave. Listen, it will be dawn when I go through the whole journey backwards, in all its details, even to the most insignificant details. But then they will possess the subtlety of refined torture.

"How mischievous it is to be born a poet! How the imagination tortures you! The sun—in beer. It sinks to the very depths of the bottle. On the opposite side of the table there is an agriculturist or someone of the sort. He has a brown face. He stirs the coffee with a green hand. Ah, my dear, they are all strangers here. There was one witness (the general), but he went away. There is still another, the ethereal one—but they don't acknowledge him. Oh, nonentities! They think they sip their sun with milk from a saucer. They do not realise that in your, in our sun their flies get stuck, the cook's saucepans clash together, the seltzer water splutters noisily and roubles tinkle sonorously on the marble table-top, like a smacking noise with the tongue. I shall go and have a look at the town. It is right out of the picture. There is the horse tramway, but it is no use. They say it is only a forty-minute walk. I found the receipt: you were right. To-morrow I doubt if I shall get there in time, I must have a good night's sleep. The day after to-morrow. Don't worry—the pawnshop is not pressing. Alas, to write is only to torture oneself. But I have not the strength to stop."

Five hours passed. There was an extraordinary silence. It became impossible to say where there was grass, where coal. A star twinkled. There was not a soul on the water-pump. In a puddle in the swampy ground the water darkened. In

150

it the reflection of a birch tree trembled. It was feverish. But very far away. Except for this, not a soul on the road.

It was extraordinarily quiet. Breathless, the engines and carriages lay on the level earth, like the accumulation of low clouds on a windless night. If it were not April the summer lightning would be playing. But the sky was restless. Surprised by a transparency, as though by an illness, sapped from within by the spring, the sky was restless. The last horse-cart belonging to the Tula tramway approached from the town. The reversible backrests of the seats banged. The last man to come out carried letters which protruded from the wide pockets of his wide great-coat. The rest went into the hall, towards a little heap of entirely strange men, noisily taking supper at the end of the room. This man remained behind the façade, searching for the green letter-box. But it was impossible to say where grass ended, where coal began, and when the tired pair of horses dragged the shaft over the turf, harrowing the track, no dust was visible and only the stable lantern gave an obscure conception of what was happening. Out of its throat the night uttered a long-drawn cry, and then everything grew silent. Far, far away, beyond the horizon.

"Tula, the 10th (deleted), the 11th, one o'clock at night. Darling, look up the textbook. You must have Kliuchevsky.[1] I put it in the suitcase myself. I don't know how to begin. I understand nothing. How strange, how fearful! While I am writing to you everything follows its normal course at the other end of the table. They behave like geniuses, they declaim and bandy phrases with one another, theatrically flinging down their serviettes on the table immediately after wiping their clean-shaven lips. But I did not say who they were. The worst appearance of bohemianism. (Carefully crossed out.) A cinematographic

[1] Famous Russian historian.—*Translator's Note.*

company from Moscow. They were staging *The Time of Troubles* in the Kremlin and wherever there were ramparts.

"Read in Kliuchevsky the episode about Petr Bolotnikov. (I think it must be there, but I haven't read it.) It brought them to Upa river. I learned later that the setting was exactly accurate, and they took the film from the opposite bank. Now the seventeenth century has been pushed into their suitcases and all the remnants linger over the untidy table. The Polish women are terrible and the boyar children are even worse! Dear friend, I am sick. This is an exhibition of the ideals of the age. The steam they are raising is mine, our common steam. This is the burning smell of ignorance and unhappy insolence. It is myself. Darling, I have sent you two letters. I don't remember them. Here is a glossary of them (crossed out, nothing substituted). Here is the glossary: genius, poet, *ennui*, verses, lack of talent, *petit bourgeois*, tragedy, woman, she, I. How terrible to see one's own defects in strangers. It is a caricature of (left unfinished)."

"2 o'clock. I swear to you that the faith of my heart is greater than ever it was, the time will come—no, let me tell you about that later. Tear me to pieces, tear me to pieces, night, burn to ashes, burn, burn brilliantly, luminously, the forgotten, the angry, the fiery word 'conscience.' (Under the word 'conscience' a line has ripped through the page.) Burn maddening, petrol-bearing tongue of flame, illuminating midnight.

"This way of regarding life has come into being and now there is no place on earth where a man can warm his soul with the fire of shame: shame is everywhere watered down and cannot burn. Falsehood and confused dissipation. Thus for thirty years all who are singular live and drench their shame, old and young, and already it has spread through the whole world, among the unknown. For

152

the first time, for the first time since the days of my child-hood, I am consumed (the whole sentence crossed out)."

One more attempt. This letter was not posted.

"How shall I describe it to you? I must begin from the end. Or else I shall never write it at all. And now permit me to talk in the third person. I wrote to you about a man who was walking past the luggage-office? Well. The poet, henceforward inscribing this word, until it is purged with fire, in inverted commas, the 'poet' observes himself in the unseemly behaviour of the actors, in the disgraceful spectacle which accuses his comrades and his generation. Perhaps he is only playing with the idea. No. They confirm him in the belief that his identity is in no way chimerical. They rise and move towards him. 'Colleague, could you give me change for three roubles?' He dispels the error. Not only actors shave. Here are twenty copecks for three roubles. He gets rid of the actor. But the affair doesn't depend on shaven lips. 'Colleague,' said the scarecrow. Yes. It is true. This is an affidavit for the prosecution. Meanwhile something new happens, a trifle, but embracing in its own way all that has happened and has been felt in the waiting-room up to this hour.

"At last the 'poet' recognises the man walking along the luggage-office. He has seen the face before. A man from the neighbourhood. He has seen him once, frequently in the course of a single day, at different times, at different places. It was when they were coupling the special train at Astapovo,[2] with a goods truck for the coffin, and when crowds of unknown people separated from the station into different trains, twirling and clawing all day according to the unexpectedness of the confused railway junction, where four railway lines meet, disperse and intercept on the return.

[2] Tolstoy died in the station-master's house at Astapovo.—
Translator's Note.

"Here a momentary consideration hovers over everything that has happened to the 'poet' in the waiting-room, like the lever which makes the revolving stage turn round, and in this way: he realises that this is Tula, this night is a night in Tula, a night in places associated with Tolstoy. No wonder the magnetic needles begin to dance here! Everything that happens happens from the nature of the place. This is an event on the *territory of conscience*, it occurs on her own ore-bearing regions. There will be no 'poet.' He swears to you, he swears to you that whenever he sees *The Time of Troubles* on the screen (that is, whenever the film is shown)—the scenes of Upa will find him utterly lonely, unless the actors become better actors, and having once trampled for a whole day over the mined regions of the spirit, they will not remain intact within their ignorance and swagger, these 'dreamers' . . ."

While these lines were being written small oil-lamps emerged from the linesmen's boxes and started creeping along the tracks. Whistles began to be heard. The railway woke up. The bruised chains screamed. Trucks were quietly sliding past the platform. They had been moving past for a long time, and they were so many that it was impossible to count them. Beyond them there gathered the approaching arrival of something breathing heavily, something obscure which belonged to the night. Because, inch by inch, behind the locomotive, there came the sudden cleansing of the roads, the unexpected appearance of night on the horizon of the empty platform, the apparition of silence along the whole breadth of semaphores and stars—the approach of the quiet countryside. This moment yawned in the rear of the goods train, bending low under a low awning, approached and slipped away.

While these lines were being written they began to couple the carriages for the train for Eletz.

The man who had been writing went on to the platform. Night lay over the whole length of the moist Russian conscience. Lanterns illuminated it. Bending over the rails, there slowly passed the goods trucks where winnowing machines lay under tarpaulins. Shadows tramped it underfoot, and the tattered steam deafened it, escaping from the valves like cockerels. The man who had been writing walked round the station. He moved behind the façade.

Nothing changed in the whole field of conscience while these lines were being written. It smelt of putrefaction and clay. Far away, at its other end, a birch tree gleamed and the runnel could be seen like a falling ear-ring. Escaping from the waiting-room, stripes of light fell on the trainway floor under the benches. And these stripes fought one another. The rumbling of beer, madness and stench, fell under the benches behind them. And still, whenever the station windows grew quiet, somewhere in the neighbourhood there could be heard the sounds of crackling and snoring. The man who had been writing walked up and down. He thought of many things. He thought of his own art, of how to find the right way. He forgot whom he had come with, whom he was seeing home, to whom he was writing. He imagined that everything would begin when he ceased listening to himself and a complete physical silence would fill his soul. Not in the manner of Ibsen, but acoustically.

So he thought. Shivers ran down his body. The east turned grey, and over the face of the whole conscience, still immersed in deep night, there fell the quick and embarrassed dew. It was time to think of getting a ticket. Cocks crowed and the booking-office woke up.

II

Then only did an extraordinarily strange old man finally go to bed in the furnished rooms in the Posolskaya. While

155

letters were being written in the station, the room shook with his light steps, and a candle in the window often ensnared the whisper which was continually being interrupted by silence. It was not the voice of the old man, although there was no other person in the room. It was all very strange.

The old man had lived through an extraordinary day. With an expression of perfect grief he left the meadow when he realised that it was not a play, but a free fantasy, which would become a play only when it was shown at the cinema. On first looking at the boyars and voivodes wavering on the farther bank, and the dark people who were leading men roped together, knocking their hats off their heads, into the nettles; on first looking at the Poles grappling up the slope behind clumps of broom, and their axes which were insensible to the sun and gave no sound, the old man began to rummage through his own repertoire. He found no histories like this. Then he came to the conclusion that it all happened four or five lifetimes ago, at the time of Ozerov and Sumarokov.[3] Then they showed him the cameraman and mentioning the cinema, an institution which he despised wholeheartedly, they reminded him that he was old and alone, of another age. He went away, grief-stricken.

He walked in his old nankeens, realising that there was no one in the world to call him Savvushka. It was a holiday. It basked in the sunlight, on sunflower seeds spread over the ground.

They spat upon it afresh with their low chesty speech. High up in the sky the ball of the moon was becoming porous, and melting away. The sky seemed cold and strangely distant. Their voices had been oiled by the things

[3] Dramatic authors of the eighteenth century.—*Translator's Note.*

156

they had eaten and drunk. Brown mushrooms, rye loaves, lard and vodka impregnated even the echo which was fading on the other bank. Several streets were crowded. Coarse flounces added a special motley to the skirts and the women.

The bushy weeds in the fields kept pace with the people walking by. Dust flew in the air, clinging to their eyes and covering the burdocks beating against the wattles and sticking to people's clothes. His cane was like a fragment of senile sclerosis. He leaned on this prolongation of his knotted veins convulsively and with gouty tightness.

.   .   .   .

All day he was full of the sensation that he had been visiting an excessively noisy rag-fair. It was one of the consequences of the play. It left unsatisfied his longing for the human speech of tragedy. This reticent hiatus sang in the ears of the old man.

All day he was ill because he had not heard a single pentameter from the shore.

And when night fell he sat by the table, held his head in his hands and remained deep in thought. He came to the conclusion that this was his death. It bore no resemblance to his past years, which were bitter and even-flowing, this inward struggle. He decided to take the medals from the cupboard and to warn someone, the door-keeper—no matter whom—but meanwhile he went on sitting there, hoping that it was nothing and would pass away.

The horse tramway tinkled as it passed. It was the last tram going to the station.

Half an hour passed. A star gleamed. Otherwise there was not a soul about. It was already late. A candle was burning, trembling. The soft silhouette of the bookcase, composed of four dark and flowing lines, rose in waves.

157

Meanwhile the night uttered a long-drawn throaty sound. Far away. In the street a door banged and people began talking agitatedly, in voices becoming to the spring evening, where there is no one about, and only a light in the room upstairs, and the window open.

The old man rose to his feet. He was transfigured. At last. He discovered something. Himself and the girl. They were helping him. And he threw himself forward, with the intention of helping these vague suggestions, so that he would not miss *both*, so that they would not disappear, so that he could cling to them and remain with them for ever. With a few steps he reached the door, half closing his eyes and waving one of his hands and hiding his chin in the other. He remembered. Suddenly he stood erect and walked bravely back, using strange steps which were not his own. Apparently he was acting.

"O, the snowstorm, the snowstorm, Lyubov Petrovna!" he exclaimed, and he spat and dribbled into his handkerchief, and again: "O, the snowstorm, Lyubov Petrovna!" he exclaimed, and this time he did not even begin to cough and achieved the likeness.

He began to move his hands and beat the air, as though he was coming in from the storm, as though he was removing his scarves and taking off his fur coat. He waited for the reply from behind the partition, and as though he could not wait any longer, he said: "Why, aren't you at home, Lyubov Petrovna?" always in the same strange voice, and he shivered when, as he *anticipated*, after an interval of twenty-five years, he heard behind the partition *over there* the gay and beloved voice: "At ho-o-me!" Then once again, and this time in exactly the same voice, with the strength of an illusion which would have increased the pride of a colleague in a similar situation, he reached out his hand, as though hovering over his tobacco-pouch, and with an oblique survey of the partition mumbled disconnectedly: "Ma-m—I—am so sorry, Lyubov Petrovna—but isn't Savva Ignatevich at home?"

It was too much. He saw both of them. Himself and the girl. Noiseless sobbing stifled the old man. Hours passed. He wept and whimpered. There was an extraordinary silence. And while the old man shuddered and helplessly dabbed his face and eyes with a handkerchief, and trembled and crumpled it, shaking his head and beating the air with his hands, like someone giggling, like someone who had choked and was surprised because, God forgive him, he was still whole and the experience had not shattered him—on the railway they began to couple the carriages for Eletz.

·　　·　　·　　·　　·

For a whole hour he conserved in tears, as in spirits, his own youth, and when the tears came to an end, everything dissolved, whirled away, vanished. He at once faded away, as though covered with dust. And then sighing, as with a guilty conscience and yawning, he went to bed.

·　　·　　·　　·　　·

He also shaved his moustache, like everyone else in the story. Like the hero, he was searching for a physical silence. In the story he was the only one to find it, compelling a stranger to speak with his own lips.

·　　·　　·　　·　　·

The train moved in the direction of Moscow and here the huge crimson sun shone on a multitude of somnolent bodies. Only a moment ago the sun appeared from behind a hill and rose high in the air.

(1918)

Translated by Robert Payne

THE CHILDHOOD OF LUVERS

THE LONG DAYS

I

Luvers was born and grew up in Perm. As once her boats and dolls, so later her memories were seeped in the shaggy bearskins of which the house was full. Her father was the director of the Luniev mineworks and possessed a large clientele among the manufacturers of Chussovaya.

The bearskins were presents, sumptuous and of a dark russet colour. The white she-bear in the child's room was like an immense chrysanthemum shedding its petals. This was the fur acquired for 'Zhenitchka's room'—chosen, paid for after long bargaining in the shop and sent along by messenger.

In summer they lived in a country house on the farther side of Kama river. In those days Zhenia was sent to bed early. She could not see the lights of Motovilikha. But once the angora cat for some reason took fright, stirred sharply in its sleep and woke up Zhenia. Then she saw grown-up people on the balcony. The alder hanging over the balustrade was thick and iridescent, like ink. The tea in the glasses was red. Cuffs and cards—yellow, the sheet —green. It was like a nightmare, but a nightmare with a name which was known to Zhenia: they were playing cards.

But on the other hand it was absolutely impossible to distinguish what was happening on the other bank in the far distance: it had no name, no clearly defined colour or sharp outine: in its motions it was familiar and dear to her and was not the nightmare, it was not that which rumbled and rolled in clouds of tobacco smoke, throwing fresh and windstrewn shadows on the reddish beams of the gallery. Zhenia began to cry. Her father came in and explained everything. The English governess turned to the wall. Her father's explanation was brief. It was—Motovilikha. You ought to be ashamed. A big girl like you. Sleep. The girl understood nothing and contentedly sucked at a falling tear. She wanted only one thing, to know the name of the unknowable—Motovilikha. That night it explained everything, for during the night the name still possessed a complete and reassuring significance for the child.

But in the morning she began to ask questions about what was Motovilikha and what happened here at night, and she learnt that Motovilikha was a factory, a government factory where castings were made and from castings . . . but all this no longer interested her and she wanted to know whether there were certain countries called 'factories' and who lived in them; but she did not ask these questions and for some reason concealed them on purpose.

And that morning she ceased to be the child she had been the previous night. For the first time in her life it occurred to her that there were things which the phenomenon conceals from people and reveals only to those who know how to shout and punish, smoke and close doors with keys. For the first time, as with this new Motovilikha, she did not say everything she thought and concealed for her own use all that was most essential, necessary and disturbing.

Years passed. From their births the children were so accustomed to their father's absences that in their eyes paternity was endowed with the special property of rarely coming to dinner and never to supper. More and more often they ate and quarrelled, drank and ate in completely empty, tenantless rooms, and the tepid lessons of the English governess could not take the place of the presence of a mother who filled the house with the sweet anguish of her vehemence and obstinacy, which was like some familiar electricity. The quiet northern day streamed through the curtains. It did not smile. The sideboard of oak grew grey hairs. The silver lay in severe and heavy piles. The hands of the English governess, washed in lavender water, moved over the table-cloth: she never gave anyone less than his proper share and possessed inexhaustible reserves of patience, and in her the sentiment of equity was as familiar as the fact that her room and her books were always clean and well-arranged. The servant who had brought one of the courses waited in the dining-room and went to the kitchen only for the next course. Everything was pleasant and agreeable, though terribly sad.

In the same way as the girl suffered years of suspicion and loneliness, of a sense of guilt and of what I would like to call *christianisme*, because it is impossible to call it christianity, so it sometimes seemed to her that nothing would or could improve, because of her depravity and impenitence; that it was all deserved. Meanwhile—but this never reached the consciousness of the children—meanwhile, on the contrary, their whole beings quivered and fermented, bewildered by the attitude of their parents towards them when their father and mother were at home; when they entered the house rather than returned home.

Their father's rare jokes generally came to grief and were always irrelevant. He felt this and felt that the children knew it. An expression of mournful confusion never left his face. When he was irritable he became a complete stranger; wholly strange at the moment when he lost control over himself. A stranger rouses no sensations. The children never answered him insolently.

But for some time the criticism which came from the children's room and silently expressed itself in their eyes made no impression on him. He failed to notice it. Invulnerable, unrecognisable, pitiable—*this* father inspired horror, unlike the irritated father—the stranger. In this way he affected the daughter more than the son. But their mother bewildered them both.

She loaded them with caresses and heaped presents on them and spent hours with them when they least desired her presence, when it crushed their childish consciences, because they felt they were undeserving; and they failed to recognise themselves in the endearing nicknames which her instinct carelessly lavished on them.

And often, when a rare and pellucid peace took possession of their souls, when they felt that they were in no way criminals, when all the secrecy which disdains discovery and resembles the fever before the rash had left them, they saw their mother as a stranger who avoided them and became angry without reason. The postman arrived. The letter was taken to the addressee—their mother. She took it without thanking them. "Go to your room." The door banged. They silently hung their heads and went out, giving way to an interminable and bewildered despair.

At first they would cry; then, after a more than usually brutal quarrel, they took fright. As years passed, this fear changed into a smouldering animosity which took deeper and deeper root.

Everything that came to the children from their parents came from afar, at the wrong moment, provoked not by them but by causes which were foreign to them; they were coloured with remoteness, as always happens, and mystery, as at night the distant howling when everyone goes to bed.

163

These were the circumstances of the children's education. They did not perceive this; for there are few, even among grown-ups, who understand what it is that forms, creates and binds them together. Life rarely tells what she is going to do with them. She loves her purpose too well, and even when she speaks of her work, it is only to those who wish her success and admire her tools. No one can help her; anyone can throw her into confusion. How? In this way. If you entrusted a tree with the care of its own growth, it would become all branch or disappear wholly into its roots or squander itself on a single leaf, forgetting that the universe must be taken as a model; and after producing one thing in a thousand, it would begin to reproduce one thing a thousand times.

So that there shall be no dead branches in the soul, so that its growth shall not be retarded, so that man shall be incapable of mingling his narrow mind with the creation of his immortal essence, there exists a number of things to turn his vulgar curiosity away from life, which does not wish to work in his presence and in every way avoids him. . . . Hence all respectable religions, all generalisations, all prejudices and the most amusing and brilliant of them all —psychology.

The children were no longer in their infancy. Ideas of punishment, retribution, reward and justice had already penetrated into their souls and diverted their senses, allowing life to do with them all it thought necessary, essential and beautiful.

II

Miss Hawthorn would not have done it. But one day, in a fit of irrational tenderness towards her children, Madame Luvers spoke sharply to the English governess over a matter of no importance at all; and the governess disappeared. Shortly afterwards she was imperceptibly replaced by a consumptive French girl. Later Zhenia remembered only that the French girl resembled a fly and no one loved her. Her name became entirely lost, and Zhenia could not say among what syllables and sounds it would be possible to find the name. All she could remember was that the French girl had scolded her, reached for the scissors and cut off the place in the bear's fur which was covered with blood.

It seemed to her that henceforward everyone would scream at her and she must suffer continual headaches and never again be able to understand that page of her favourite book which became so stupidly confused before her eyes, like a lesson-book after dinner.

The day drew out its terrible length. Her mother was away. She was not sorry. She even imagined she was glad her mother was away.

Soon the long day was given over to oblivion among the tenses of *passé* and *futur antérieur*: watering the hyacinths and strolling along the Sibirskaya and Okhanskaya. So well forgotten that Zhenia neither felt nor paid any attention to the length of that other day, the second in her life, when she read in the evening by the light of a lamp and the indolent progress of the story inspired her with a thousand futile thoughts. And when, much later, she remembered the house in the Ossinskaya where they lived, she thought of it always as she had seen it on that second long day which was coming to an end. A day without end. Spring outside. Spring in the Urals, so ill and so laboriously brought to fruition, then breaking loose wildly and tempestuously in the course of a single night, then flowing in a wild tempestuous stream. The lamps only stressed the insipidity of the evening air. They gave no light but

165

swelled from within, like diseased fruit, from the clear and lustreless dropsy which dilated their swollen shades. They were absent. One came upon them precisely where they should be, in their places on the tables, and they hung from the sculptured ceilings of the rooms where the girl was accustomed to see them. Yet the lamps possessed fewer points of contact with the rooms than with the spring sky, to which they seemed to have been brought so close, like a glass of water to the bed of a sick man. Their souls were in the street where, on a level with the humid earth, there crawled the gossip of servant girls and drops of melting snow, continually thinning out, congealed for the night. It was there that the lamps disappeared for the evening. Her parents were away. But it appeared that her mother was expected that day. That long day or the day afterwards. Probably. Or perhaps she arrived suddenly, inadvertently. That too was possible.

Zhenia went to bed and saw that the day had been long for the same reason as before, and at first she thought of getting the scissors and cutting away those places on her princess-slip and on the sheets, but later she decided to get the French governess's powder and whiten the stains; and she was holding the powder box in her hands when the governess came in and slapped her. 'She powders herself. The only thing that was wanting. Now she understood everything. She had noticed it long ago.' Zhenia burst into tears, because she had been slapped, because she had been scolded, because she was offended and because, knowing that she was innocent of the crime imputed to her by the governess, she knew she was guilty—she felt it—of something which exceeded the governess's suspicions. It was necessary—she felt this urgently and with a sense of stupefaction—felt it in her temples and in her knees—it was necessary to conceal it, without knowing how or why, but

166

somehow and at whatever the cost. Her joints moved painfully with a suggestion of interrupted hypnotism. And this suggestion, agonising and wearying, was itself the work of that organism which concealed from the girl the significance of what had happened to her, and being itself the criminal, made her see in her bleeding a disgusting and distasteful sin. 'Menteuse!' She was compelled to content herself with a denial, concealing stubbornly that which was worse than anything, standing half-way between the shame of illiteracy and the ignominy of a scandal in the streets. She shivered and clenched her teeth, stifling her sobs, she pressed herself against the wall. She could not throw herself into the Kama because it was still cold, and the last vestiges of ice were floating down the river.

Neither the girl nor the governess heard the bell in time. Their mutual excitement disappeared in the silence of the russet-coloured bearskins; and when her mother came in, it was too late. She found her daughter in tears, the governess—blushing. She demanded an explanation. The governess explained brutally that—not Zhenia, but votre enfant, she said—her child was powdering herself and she had noticed it and suspected it long ago—the mother refused to let her finish the sentence—her terror was unfeigned—the child not yet thirteen. "Zhenia—you?—my God, what have you come to?" (At that moment her mother imagined that her words were intelligent, as though she had realised long ago that her daughter was disgracing herself and becoming depraved, but she had made no efforts to prevent it—and now her daughter was descending into the depths.) "Zhenia, tell me the truth—it will be worse—what were you doing—with the powder-box?" is probably what Madame Luvers wanted to say, but instead she said, "With this thing?" and she seized 'this thing' and brandished it in the air. "Mama, don't believe mam'zelle, I never——" and she burst into tears. But her mother heard evil notes behind the tears; where there were none. She felt that she was herself to blame and suffered from an inward terror: it was necessary, she thought, to remedy everything, even though it was against her maternal instinct 'to rise to pedagogic and reasonable measures.' She resolved not to yield to compassion. She decided to wait until the tears, which wounded her deeply, came to an end.

And she sat on the bed, gazing quietly and vacantly at the edge of the bookshelf. There came from her the odour of costly perfume. When the child grew quiet, she began to question her again. Zhenia, her eyes brimming with tears, stared out of the window and whimpered. Ice was coming down, probably with a shattering sound. A star was glimmering. And there was the rugged darkness of the empty night, cold, clear-cut, lustreless. Zhenia looked away from the window. In her mother's voice she heard the menace of impatience. The French governess stood against the wall, all gravity and concentrated pedagogy. Her hand with an adjutant's gesture lay on the ribbon of her watch. Once more Zhenia turned towards the stars and Kama river. She decided. In spite of the cold, in spite of the ice. She—dived. She lost herself in her words, her terrible and inaccurate words, and told her mother about the thing. Her mother let her speak to the end only because she was astounded by the warmth with which the child coloured her confession. Everything became clear from the first word. No; from the moment when the child swallowed a deep gulp of air before she began her story. She listened in an anguish of love and tenderness for the slender body. She wanted to throw herself on her daughter's neck and burst into tears. But—pedagogy; she rose from the bed and lifted the counterpane. She called her daughter to her and began to stroke her head slowly, slowly, tenderly. "You've been a good girl . . ." the words tumbled out of her mouth. Noisily she went to the window and turned away from them. Zhenia did not see the governess. Her tears—her mother—filled the room. "Who makes the bed?" The question was senseless. The girl trembled. She was sorry for Grusha. Then unknown words, in familiar French, came to her ears: they were speaking angrily. And then once more in a different voice, "Zhenitchka, my child, go into the dining-room, I shall be there in a minute. I shall tell you about the beautiful country house we have taken for you in the summer—for you and your father in the summer."

The lamps became simple again, as in winter, at home, with the Luvers—warm, zealous, faithful. Her mother's sable moved playfully over the blue woollen tablecloth. *"Won am holding to Blagodat wait end Passion Week unless,"*—impossible to read the rest, the end of the telegram was folded. Zhenia sat down on the edge of the divan, tired and happy. She sat down modestly and comfortably, just as six months later in the corridor of the school in Ekaterinburg she sat on the edge of a cold yellow bench and when she had finished her *viva voce* in the Russian language and received the highest marks she knew that she could go.

.   .   .   .   .

The next morning her mother told her what to do when *this thing* happened to her, it was nothing, she mustn't be afraid, it would happen again. She mentioned nothing by name and explained nothing, but added that from now on she herself would prepare her daughter's lessons, because she was never going away again.

The French governess was removed on the grounds of negligence after spending only a few months in the family.

When the carriage was ordered for her and she was coming down the stairs, she met the doctor who was coming up on the landing. He replied to her greeting coldly, saying nothing at all about her departure; she suspected that he knew everything; she scowled and shrugged her shoulders.

The maid was waiting for the doctor at the door, while in the hall where Zhenia was standing the murmur of footsteps and the murmur of ringing flagstones echoed longer than usual in the air. And this was the memory which always impressed itself upon her when she thought of her early puberty: the shrill echo of the chirping streets in the morning, hesitating on the stairs, joyfully penetrating into the house; the French governess, the maid and the doctor, the two criminals and the one who was initiated, cleansed, made immune by the light, by the freshness of air and the resonance of footsteps.

The warm April sun was shining. 'Feet, meet, wipe your feet!' from end to end echoed the bright and empty corridor. The furs were removed for the summer. The rooms were clear and transfigured, they sighed with relief and with sweetness. All that day, all that long day which wearily drew out its long length, without end, in all the corners, in all the rooms, in the glass sloping against the wall,[1] in mirrors, in tumblers full of water, in the blue air of the garden, bird-cherry and choking, foaming honeysuckle smiled and raved, blinking and burnishing themselves, insatiable, unquenchable. The tedious conversations of the courtyards lasted all day: they announced that the night was dethroned and all day long they repeated incessantly in *roulades* that acted like a sleeping-draught that there would be no more evening and they would let no one

[1] The outer panes of glass from double windows are removed during the summer and in this case were still left against the wall. —*Translator's Note.*

sleep. 'Feet, feet!'—but they burnt as they came in, drunk with air, with the sound in the ears, and therefore they failed to understand clearly what was being said and strove to finish the meal as quickly as they could, so that, when they moved away their chairs with a tremendous noise, they could run backwards once more into this day, which was breaking impetuously on the time reserved for evening, into this day, in which the tree drying in the sun gave forth its exiguous chant and the blue sky chattered piercingly and the earth shone greasily, like a swamp. The frontier between the house and the courtyard vanished. The rag did not rub all the traces away. The floors were covered with a dry and brilliant dust, and crackled.

Her father had brought sweets and miracles. The house was marvelously pleasant. With a moist rustle the stones announced their appearance from the tissue-paper which gradually assumed their colour and became more and more transparent as layer after layer of the white paper, as soft as gauze, was removed. Some of the stones resembled drops of almond milk, others resembled splashes of blue water-colour, still others were like solidified tears of cheese. Some were blind, sleepy, full of dreams; others sparked gaily with the sparkle of the frozen juice of blood oranges. No one desired to touch them. They were perfect as they were, as they emerged from the froth of paper which secreted them, like a plum secreting its lustreless juice.

The father was unusually gentle with the children and often accompanied their mother into the town. They would return together, and they appeared to be happy. But the important thing was that they were both quiet and gentle and even-tempered, and when at odd moments their mother gazed into the eyes of the father with an air of playful reproach, it was as though she was deriving a sense of peace from his small and ugly eyes, and then pouring it

171

out again from her own eyes, which were large and beautiful, on her children and those who were near her.

Once her parents rose very late. Then, no one knows why, they decided to take lunch on the steamer which lay off the landing-stage, and they took the children with them. They let Seriozha taste the cold beer. They enjoyed themselves so much that they decided to have lunch on the steamer again. The children did not recognise their parents. What had happened? The daughter was blissfully, perplexedly happy, and it seemed to her that life would always be as it was then. They did not grieve when they learned that they were not going to the country house that summer. Their father left shortly afterwards. Three huge yellow travelling trunks, with durable metal rims, appeared at the house.

III

The train left late at night. Luvers came over a month earlier and wrote that the flat was ready. Several *izvoschiks* were driving to the station at a trot. They knew they were near the station by the colour of the pavement. The pavement was black and the street-lamps lashed at the brown railway. Meanwhile from the viaduct a view opened upon Kama river, while under them rattled and ran a soot-black pit, heavy with gravity and terror. It ran off, swift as lightning, until finally in the far distance it took fright, trembled and went gliding among the twinkling beads of distant signals.

The wind rose. The silhouettes of houses and walls flew upwards, like chaff from a sieve; they twirled and their ends frayed in the friable air. There was the smell of mashed potatoes. Their *izvoschik* edged away from the line of rocking baskets and carriage-backs in front, and began to outstrip them. From a distance they recognised the cart which was carrying their luggage; they ran alongside; Ulyasha shouted something to her mistress from the cart, but whatever she said was lost in the rattle of wheels, and she shivered and jolted, and her voice jolted.

The daughter perceived no sorrow in the novelty of all these night sounds and darkness and the freshness of air. For in the distance there was something mysterious and black. Beyond the dockside warehouses lights—the town rinsed them in water—were dangling from the shore and from ships. Then many more appeared, swarming in black clusters, greasily, blind like maggots. On Lyubimovsky wharf the funnels, the roofs of the warehouses and the decks were a sober blue. Barges stared at the stars. "This is a rat-hole," Zhenia thought. White porters surrounded them. Seriozha was the first to jump down. He glanced round and was extremely surprised when he noticed that the cart with their luggage was already there—the horse threw back her head, her collar rose, reared up like a cock, she pressed on the back of the cart and began to move backwards. But throughout the journey Seriozha was pre-occupied with the thought of how far the cart would remain behind them.

The boy, intoxicated with the prospect of the journey, stood there in his white school shirt. The journey was a novelty for them both, and already he knew and loved those words: depot, loco, siding, through-carriage, and the marriage of sounds: 'class' had a sour-sweet taste in his mouth. His sister was also enthusiastic in all this, but in her own way, without the boyish love of method which characterised the enthusiasm of her brother.

Suddenly, as though from under the ground, his mother appeared. She ordered the children to be taken to the buffet. From there, threading her way proudly through the crowds, she went straight to the man who was called, as loudly and threateningly as possible, for the first time, 'the stationmaster'—a name which was to be mentioned often in different places, with variations and among different crowds.

A yawn conquered them. They sat at one of the windows which were so dusty, so starchy and so vast that they appeared to be institutions of bottle-glass, where it was impossible to remain with a hat on one's head. The girl saw: behind the glass not a street but a room, only more solemn and morose than the one in the decanter before her; and into this room steam-engines moved slowly and came to a pause, bringing the darkness with them; but when they had left the room, it seemed that it was not a room, for there was the sky behind the columns and on the other side—a rolling meadow and wooden houses and there were people walking about, fading into the distance; where perhaps cocks are now crowing and not long ago the water-carrier left pools of water . . .

It was a provincial railway station without the glow and hurly-burly of the capital, where people came together in good time when they leave the city shrouded in night, with long waiting and silence and wanderers who slept on the ground with hunting dogs, baggages, engines wrapped up in straw and uncovered bicycles.

The children lay on the upper seat. The boy fell asleep at once. The train was still standing in the station. It grew bright, and suddenly the girl realised that the carriage was clean, dark blue, cold. And gradually she realised—but she was already asleep.

.   .   .   .   .

He was a very fat man. He read the newspaper and swayed from side to side. As soon as you looked at him, the swaying became obvious—in which everything in the carriage was flooded and impregnated, as with sunshine.

174

Zhenia regarded him from above with the lazy precision with which a man thinks about things or looks at things who is fresh and wholly awake and who lies in bed only because he is waiting, because the decision to get up will come of its own accord, without assistance, clear and unconstrained like his other thoughts. She watched the fat man and thought, where did he enter the carriage and how did he manage to be already washed and dressed? She had no idea of the time. She had only just wakened, therefore it was morning. She looked at him, but he could not see her: her upper berth was inclined deep against the wall. He did not see her because he rarely glanced from his newspaper, upwards, sideways, crosswise—and when he lifted his head towards her bed, their eyes did not meet and either he saw only the mattress or else . . . but she quickly tucked them under herself and pulled on her scanty stockings. Mama was in the corner over there. She was already dressed and reading a book, Zhenia decided reflectively as she studied the eyes of the tubby man. But Seriozha was not beneath her? Where was he? And she yawned sweetly and stretched herself. The terrible heat— she had realised it only that very moment, and she turned away from the heads and peered into the small window which was at half mast. "But where is the earth?" she exclaimed in her heart.

What she saw is beyond description. A forest of clamorous hazel trees, into which they were poured by the serpentine train, became the sea, became the world, became anything you pleased, everything. The forest ran on, brilliantly clear, freshly murmuring, down, down the broad slopes, and growing smaller, curdling and becoming misty, it fell steeply, almost entirely black. And that which rose on the other side of the void resembled something huge, all curls and circles, a yellow-green storm-cloud plunged in

175

thought and stupefied by torpor. Zhenia held her breath, and at once perceived the speed of that limitless and forgetful air, and at once realised that the huge cloud was some country, some place bearing a sonorous and mountainous name, rolling along like a thunderstorm flung into the valley, with rocks and with sand; and the hazel trees did nothing but whisper it and whisper it; here, there and away over there; nothing else.

"Is it the Urals?" she asked of the whole compartment, leaning forward.

.   .   .   .   .

For the rest of the journey she never took her eyes away from the window in the corridor. She clung to the window and was continually leaning out. She was greedy. She discovered that it was more pleasant to look backwards than to look forward. Majestic acquaintance dimmed and disappeared into the distance. A short separation from them, in the course of which, accompanied by the vertical roar of the grinding chains and a draught of fresh air which made her neck grow cold, a new miracle appeared; and again you search for them. The mountainous panorama extended and kept on growing. Some were black, others were refreshed, some were obscured, others obscured. They came together and separated, they ascended and climbed down. All this moved in a sort of low circle, like the rotation of stars, with the prudent caution of giants anxious for the preservation of the earth, on the edge of catastrophe. These complex progressions were ruled by a level and powerful echo inaccessible to human ears and all-seeing. It watched them with eagle eye, mute and invisible; it held them under its gaze. In this way are built, built and rebuilt the Urals.

For a moment she returned to the carriage, screwing up her eyes against the harsh light. Mama was smiling and talking to the strange gentleman. Seriozha was fidgeting

176

with the crimson plush and clinging to a leather wall-strap. Mama spat the last seed into the palm of her hand, swept up the ones which had fallen on her dress and inclining nimbly and impetuously threw all the rubbish under the seat. Contrary to their expectations the fat man possessed a husky, cracked voice. He evidently suffered from asthma. Mama introduced him to Zhenia and offered her a mandarine. He was amusing and probably kind, and while talking he was continually lifting a plump hand to his mouth. He was troubled with his voice, and suddenly becoming constrained it was often intermittent. It appeared that he was from Ekaterinburg and he had often travelled through the Urals, which he knew well; and when he took his gold watch from his waistcoat pocket and lifted it to his nose and began to put it back again, Zhenia noticed that his fingers were kind. Like all fat people he seized things with a movement which suggested that he was giving them away and his hands sighed all the time as though proferred for a kiss, and they swung gently in the air, as though they were hitting a ball against the floor. "Now, it'll come soon," he murmured, looking away from the boy, although he was speaking to him, and smiling broadly.

"You know, the signpost they talk about, on the frontier of Asia and Europe, and 'Asia' written on it," Seriozha blurted out, slipping off his cushion and bolting down the corridor.

Zhenia did not understand any of this, and when the fat man explained to her what it was, she immediately ran to the same side of the carriage and looked out for the signpost, afraid that she had already missed it. In her enchanted head 'the frontier of Asia' assumed the nature of a hallucinatory borderline, like the iron balustrade placed between the public and a cage full of pumas, a menacing bar, black like the night, fraught with danger and evil-smelling. She waited for the signpost as though she was waiting for the curtain to rise on the first act of a geographical tragedy, about which she had heard rumours from witnesses, triumphantly excited because this had happened to her and because she would soon see it with her own eyes.

But meanwhile that which had compelled her to enter the compartment with the older people monotonously continued: the grey alders, past which they had been moving for half an hour were not coming to an end and nature was apparently making no preparations for that which awaited it. Zhenia became angry with dust-laden, wearisome Europe, which was clumsily holding at a distance the appearance of the miracle. And how amazed she was when, as though in reply to Seriozha's furious cry, something which resembled a gravestone flashed past the window, moved to one side and ran away, withdrawing into the alders from the alders racing after it, the long-awaited legendary name! At that moment a multitude of heads, as though in agreement, leaned out of the windows of all the carriages, while clouds of dust, borne down the slope, enlivened the train. Already they had driven some miles into Asia, but still their shawls quivered on their floating heads, and they looked at one another, and all of them, bearded or shaven, flew past, flying in clouds of whirling sand, flying past the dust-laden alders which were Europe a short while ago and were now long since Asia.

IV

Life began afresh. Milk was not brought into the house, into the kitchen, by an itinerant milkmaid; it was brought into the house every morning by Ulyasha in two pails; and the white bread was of a special kind, not like that of Perm. Here there were strange pavements resembling marble or alabaster, with a wavy white sheen. The flagstones were blinding even in the shadows, like ice-cold suns, greedily engulfing the shadows of spruce trees, which spread out, melted in them and liquefied. Here the feeling was quite different when you walked on the roads, which were wide and luminous, with trees planted in them, as in Paris—Zhenia repeated after her father.

He spoke of this on the first day of their arrival. It was a fine, spacious day. Her father had a snack meal before going to meet them at the station and took no part in the dinner. His place at the table was therefore clean and bright, like Ekaterinburg, and he only spread out his serviette and sat sideways and spoke about things in generalities. He unbuttoned his waistcoat and his shirt-front curved crisply and vigorously. He said it was a beautiful European town and rang the bell when it was necessary to take the dishes away and order something else, and he rang the bell and continued talking. And along the unknown paths of the still unknown rooms a noiseless white maid came to them, a brunette, all starch and flounces, and they said 'you' to her, and this maid—this new maid smiled at the mistress and the children, as though they were old acquaintances. And this maid was admonished with various injunctions about Ulyasha, who found herself there, in an unknown and probably very dark kitchen where certainly there was a window which looked out upon something new: some steeple or other or a rod or birds. And Ulyasha would at once begin to ask questions of the girl, putting on her worst clothes, so that she could do the unpacking afterwards; she would ask questions and become familiar with things and look: in which corner was the stove, in that one, as in Perm, or elsewhere?

The boy learned from his father that they were not far from the school—indeed it was quite near—and they could not avoid seeing it as they drove past; the father drank up his *narzan*,[2] swallowed and continued: "Is it possible I didn't show it to you? You don't see it from here, from the kitchen probably. (He weighed it in his mind.) But only the roof——" and he drank up the *narzan* and rang the bell.

The kitchen was cool and bright, exactly—as it at once appeared to the girl—as she had imagined it in the dining-room,—a kitchen-range with tiles painted blue and white, and there were two windows in the place she had expected them: Ulyasha threw something on her bare arms, the room became full of childish voices, people were walking along the roof of the school and the topmost scaffolding protruded. "Yes, it's being repaired," father said, when they came in one after another, noisily thrusting their way into the dining-room through the already known but still unexplored corridor, which she would have to visit again on the following day, after unpacking her exercise books and hanging up her face flannel on the wall and finishing a thousand things.

"Wonderful butter," mother said, sitting down; and they went into the classroom which they had already visited, still wearing their hats as they entered. "Why should it all be Asia?" she thought aloud. But Seriozha did not understand that which he would understand perfectly at another time, for until now they had lived and thought in unison. He swung towards the map hanging on the wall and moved his hand downwards along the Ural mountains, looking at his sister, smitten, so it seemed to him, by his argument. "They agreed to trace a natural frontier, that's all!" And she remembered the noon of that same day, already so far away. It was unbelievable that a day which

[2] A kind of mineral water.—*Translator's Note.*

had contained all this—this day, now in Ekaterinburg, and still here—had not yet come to an end. At the thought of all that had fled past, preserving its breathless order, into the predestined distance, she experienced a sensation of amazing tiredness, the sensation which the body experiences in the evening after a laborious day. As though she had taken part in the removal and displacement of all this burden of loveliness, and had strained herself. And for some reason assured that it existed, her Urals, *over there*, she turned and ran into the kitchen across the dining-room where there was less crockery, but where there was still the wonderful iced butter on the damp maple-leaves and the sour mineral water.

The school was being repaired and the air, like linen on the teeth of the sempstress, was ripped by shrill martins and down below—she leaned out of the window—a carriage gleamed in front of the open coachhouse and sparks flew up from a grinding-wheel and there was the smell of food which has been eaten, a finer and more interesting smell than when it was being served, a long-lasting melancholy smell, as in a book. She forgot why she was running and did not notice that her Urals were not in Ekaterinburg, but she did notice how they were singing below, underneath, while they were working at their easy tasks (probably washing the floors and spreading bast with warm hands) and how they were splashing the water from the kitchen-pails and how, although they were splashing downstairs, how quiet it was everywhere! And how the tap babbled, and how: "Well, my dear"; but she still avoided the new girl and had no wish to hear her—and how—she pursued her thoughts to the end—everyone underneath them knew and indeed said: "There are people in number two now." Ulyasha entered the kitchen.

The children slept soundly during their first night, and

181

they woke up: Seriozha in Ekaterinburg, Zhenia in Asia, as once more it occurred to her, strangely and with certainty. Flakes of alabaster were playing lightly on the ceiling.

.   .   .   .   .

This began while it was yet summer. They declared to her that she had to go to school. This was in no way unpleasant. But they *declared* it to her. She did not call the tutor into the schoolroom, where the sunlight clung so closely to the colour-wash wall that in the evening it succeeded in tearing off the adhesive day only with bloodshed. She did not call him when, accompanied by her mother, he went there to make the acquaintance of 'his future pupil.' It was not she who gave him the absurd name of Dikikh. Nor was it she who wished that henceforward the soldiers would always be taught at noon, immense, shaggy, wheezing, perspiring like the convulsions of a stopcock before the breakdown of the water supply; and that their thigh-boots would be squeezed by lilac-coloured storm-clouds which knew more about guns and wheels than their white shirts, white tents and officers whiter still. Was it she who wished that now there would always be two things: a small basin and a serviette, which combined together like the carbon rods of an arc lamp and evoked a third being which momentarily evaporated: the idea of death, like those signboards at the barber's where it first occurred to her? And was it with her consent that the red turnpikes, on which it was written, "No loitering!" assumed the position of a local and forbidden secret, and the Chinese—something intimately terrible, closely related to Zhenia and horrifying? But not everything lay heavy on her soul. There were pleasant things too, like her approaching entry into the school. But all this was *declared* to her. Life ceased to be a poetical caprice; it fermented around her like a harsh and evil-coloured fable—in so far as it became prose and was transformed into fact. Stubbornly, painfully and lustrelessly, as though in a state of eternal sobering, elements of trivial existence entered into her awakening spirit. They sank deep within her, real, solid, cold: like weary pewter spoons. Here, deep down, the pewter began to melt and clot and fuse into fixed ideas.

v

Often the Belgians came to tea. So they were called. It was her father who called them this, saying: "To-day the Belgians are coming to tea." There were four of them. One, unbearded, came rarely and never talked. Sometimes he came along, by accident, during the week, choosing a rainy and uninteresting day. The other three were inseparable. Their faces resembled cakes of fresh soap, unbroken, from the wrapper, sweet-scented and cold. One wore a thick and downy beard and downy, chestnut-coloured hair. They always appeared in the company of their father, returning from some meeting or other. In the house everyone liked them. When they spoke, it was as though they were spilling water on the tablecloth: noisily, freshly, immediately, sometimes to one side where no one expected it, with the long-lingering trails of their jokes and their anecdotes, always understood by the children, always quenching their thirst and clean.

All round there was noise, the sugar-basin gleamed, the nickel-plated coffee-pot, the clean vigorous teeth, the compact linen. With mother they joked politely and courteously. And these colleagues of her father possessed an extremely fine skill in restraining him when, in reply to one of their swift innuendoes and references to things and people known at the table only to them, the professionals, her father began, with difficulty and in imperfect French, diffusely, to speak hesitatingly about contractors, about *références approuvées* and about *férocités*, i.e., *bestialités, ce qui veut dire en russe*—embezzlement at Blagodat.

For some time the beardless one had been attempting to learn Russian, and he often sought to show off his skill in his new department of knowledge; but so far with little success. One could not laugh over the French periods of her father, and all his *férocités* were seriously wearisome; but precisely because of his position, the gusts of laughter which greeted Negarat's attempts at Russian were fully justified.

They called him Negarat. He was a Walloon from the Flemish districts of Belgium. They recommended Dikikh to him. He wrote his address in Russian, amusingly transcribing the more difficult letters, such as Ю, Я, Ѣ. They came from him in duplicate, unmatched and with their legs straddled apart. The children permitted themselves to sit with their knees on the leather cushions of the armchairs, their elbows on the table—everything was permissible, everything was merged together, the Ю was not Ю but a sort of ten, everywhere there was squealing and bursting into laughter. Evans was banging the table with his fist and wiping away his tears, father was trembling and blushing, walking up and down the room and repeating, "No, I really can't!" and crumbling his handkerchief. *"Faites de nouveau!"* Evans was blowing on the flames. *"Commencez!"* and Negarat opened his mouth a little like someone who stammers and lingers for a while and wonders how he will ever be able to bring to birth those Russian syllables still unexplored, like colonies in the Congo.

"Dites, uvy, nevygodno," father suggested hoarsely, humidly, spitting out the words.

Ouivoui, niévoui. . . ."

"*Entends-tu?—ouvoui, niévoui—ouvi-niévoui—oui, oui
—chose inouie, charmant,*" the Belgians broke out laughing.

. . . . .

Summer went by. Some examinations were passed successfully, others brilliantly. The cold, transparent noises of the corridors flowed as from a fountain. Here everyone knew one another. The leaves in the garden grew yellow and gold. In their bright, dancing reflection the school windows pined away. Half-lustreless the windows became clouded over and shook at their base. The upper panes of the windows were rent by blue convulsions. The bronze branches of the maple trees ploughed across their frigid clarity.

She did not expect that all her emotions would be transformed into such pleasant mockery. Divide so many feet, so many yards by seven! Was it worth while to learn all about those ounces, pounds, quarters, stones? Or grains, drams, ounces, pounds avoirdupois—which always seemed to her to be the four ages in the life of the scorpion? Why, in the word 'useful' must you write one sort of 'e' [3] rather than another? And she worked hard over the answer, only because all her strength was concentrated in the effort of imagining the unfavourable reasons which would compel the word 'useful' with the wrong 'e' (so shaggy and wild when it is written in this way) to arise. She never knew why they did not send her to school, although she had been admitted and was enrolled, and already her coffee-coloured uniform had been tried on, avariciously and importunately, for several hours; and her room already contained many horizons: a bag, a pencil case, a luncheon basket and a remarkably loathsome india-rubber.

[3] In the old Russian orthography there were three letters for the sound expressed by the English "e."—*Translator's Note.*

The Childhood of Luvers

I

THE GIRL was swathed from head to knees in a thick woollen shawl; like a pullet she ran about in the courtyard. Zhenia wanted to go up to the Tartar girl and talk to her. At that moment a window was flung open noisily. "Kolka!" Aksinya shouted. The boy, who resembled one of those bundles the peasants carry, and into which felt shoes would have been hurriedly thrust, trotted briskly into the porter's lodge.

To take the work into the courtyard meant always having pored over a footnote to a rule until it had lost all significance, to go upstairs and begin afresh in the house. From the threshold the rooms immediately transpierced you with a peculiar semi-darkness and freshness and with an always unexpected familiarity which the furniture, having assumed once and for all its appointed place, retained. It is impossible to foretell the future. But it was possible to realise its presence as you walked into the house. Here the scheme of the future was already mapped out, the disposition of forces to which the future was subordinated, while refractory towards everything else. And there was no dream, inspired by the motion of the air in the street, which could not easily be dispersed by the quick and fatal spirit of the house, as it rushed in suddenly, from the threshold of the hall.

This time it was Lermontov. Zhenia crumpled up the book, folding it so that the binding lay inside. In the house, if Seriozha had done this, she would herself have rebelled against the 'ugly habit.' But in the courtyard it was another matter.

Prokhor laid the ice-cream freezer on the ground and went back into the house. When he opened the door into the hall, there came from thence the lolling, devilish barking of the general's short-haired house-dogs. The door slammed with a quick bang.

Meanwhile Terek, bounding up like a lioness, with a shaggy mane along her back,[1] continued to roar as he thought fit, and Zhenia began to wonder, but only about this: was it the back or the spine which was referred to? She was too lazy to look in the book, and "the golden clouds from the south, from the distance" had hardly time to follow Terek, for they were already meeting with the threshold of the general's kitchen, with a pail and a bast wisp in the hand.

The batman placed the pail on the ground, bent down, took the ice-cream freezer to pieces and began to wash it. The August sun bored through the wooden leaves and took root in the soldier's hind-quarters. Reddening, the sun embedded itself on his uniform and like turpentine greedily soaked into him.

The courtyard was wide, with intricate secluded corners, ponderous and complicated. With paving-stones in the centre, it had not been re-paved for a long time and the cobbles were overgrown with level, curly-headed grasses which gave off, in the hour after dinner, an acid, medicinal smell, like the smell of a hospital as you pass by on a hot day. At one end, between the lodge and the courtyard coach-house, the courtyard boardered upon a strange garden.

There, among the stacks of firewood, Zhenia wandered.

[1] Refers to a famous blunder in Lermontov's *Demon*. Lionesses have no manes.—*Translator's Note*.

She propped a ladder among the level faggots to prevent it from falling, she took it into the shifting wood and sat on a rung in the middle, casually and uncomfortably, as though she was playing a game in the courtyard. Then she stretched up and climbed higher, placing the book on the topmost broken rung and preparing to give her attention to the *Demon*, until she discovered that she sat more comfortably where she was before and climbed down again and forgot the book among the faggots and did not remember, because she thought only of what she had seen for the first time on the other side of the strange garden—she never previously imagined there could be such a thing behind it—she stood there gaping, like someone enchanted.

There were no bushes in the strange garden, and the ancient trees, bearing their lower branches upwards towards the leaves, as though into darkness, stripped bare the garden below, although it stood in continual shadow, solemn and open to the air, and never moving out of the shade. Forked trees, lilac-coloured during the storm and covered with a grey lichen, made it easy to see the deserted, rarely frequented street upon which the strange garden looked out on the other side. A yellow acacia tree grew there. Now it was parched, it bent down and let fall its leaves.

Transferred by the dark garden from this world to the other, the forgotten sidestreet shone brilliantly, like something in a dream; brilliantly and minutely illuminated, and noiseless, as though the sun, wearing glasses, was scrabbling in the chickweed.

But what was Zhenia gaping at? At her own discovery, which interested her more than it interested the people who were helping her to make it. Then there was a small shop there? Beyond the wicket-gate, in the street! In such a street! She envied the strangers, 'the happy ones.' There were three women.

They wore black, like the word 'nun' in the song. Three smooth napes, under their circular hats, were inclined so that it seemed that the last, half hidden by a bush, slept while leaning on something, but the other two were also asleep and drawn up close to her. Their hats were of a dark dove-grey, and they glittered in the sunlight and died out again like insects. They were covered with black crêpe. Meanwhile the strangers turned in the other direction. Obviously something at the end of the street had attracted their attention. For a few minutes they looked at the end of the street, as one looks in summer, when a second will dissolve into the light and draw out its length, when one has to screw up one's eyes and shade them with one's hands—they looked for a few moments and fell once more into their former state of unanimous somnolence.

Zhenia was just going to go in when suddenly she remembered the book, although at first she had no idea where it was. She came back for it, and when she returned to the logs, she noticed that the strangers had got up and were moving away. They were walking singly, in single file, towards the wicket-gate. A small man followed them with a strange crippled manner of walking. Under his arm he was carrying a huge album or an atlas. Now it was clear to her what they had been doing, each was looking over the shoulder of the other, and she thought—they were sleeping. The neighbours moved about in the garden and hid behind the outhouses. Already the sun was going down. Reaching up for her book, Zhenia shook the piled logs. The pile awoke and moved as though alive. Several logs flew down and fell on the grass with a light sound. This was the signal, like a night-watchman's rattle. Evening was born. Innumerable quiet and misty sounds were born. The air began to whistle a tune of long ago, of the other side of the river.

The courtyard was empty. Prokhor had finished his

work. He moved beyond the gates. Low over the grasses came the melancholy string-thrumming of a soldier's balalaika. And there spun and danced above her head, dipping and falling, and sinking, and at last without touching the earth there climbed upwards a thin swarm of silent midges. But the thrumming of the balalaika was still quieter and more tenuous. It sank to the earth below the midges, but without becoming covered in dust, more delicate and airy than the swarm, it rushed upwards into the heights, glittering and falling, in cadences, slowly.

Zhenia returned to the house. "Lame," she thought, thinking of the unknown man who carried an album. "Lame, but not a poor man, without crutches." She went into the house through the back door. From the courtyard there came the smell, cloying and persistent, of camomile. "For some time mother has almost acquired a chemist's shop, a whole collection of blue bottles with yellow stoppers." Slowly she climbed the stairs. The iron banisters were cold, the stairs gnashed in reply to her scraping feet. Suddenly a strange thought entered her head. She stepped over two stairs and came to rest on a third. It occurred to her that for some time there had existed an incomprehensible resemblance between her mother and the lodge-keeper's wife. There was something altogether elusive in this resemblance. She paused. It lay—she thought—in something people bear in mind when they are talking: we are all mortal . . . or we are all tarred with the same brush . . . or fate pays no respect to birth—she pushed the bottle, which was rolling on its side, with her foot and it flew down and fell on the dusty mat-bag without breaking—in something which was very common indeed, common to all people. But then why not go on to discover resemblances between herself and Aksinya? Or between Aksinya and Ulyasha? And it was all the more strange to Zhenia because it would be difficult to find two more dissimilar natures: in Aksinya there was something earthly as in a market-garden, something resembling swollen potatoes and the diseases of a rabid pumpkin. Whereas her mother . . . Zhenia smiled at the thought of a comparison . . .

And meanwhile it was Aksinya who gave the right note to the obtruding comparison. She became the centre of the *rapprochement* . . . The countrywoman gained nothing, but the lady lost something. A moment later something else occurred to Zhenia. It occurred to her that rusticity had already penetrated into her mother's nature, and she imagined her mother saying '*shuka*' instead of '*shchuka*,' '*rabotam*' instead of '*rabotaem*'; perhaps—it occurred to her—the day will come and she will just step in and offer a heavy peasant greeting in a new silk dressing-gown which is without a girdle.

In the corridor there was a smell of medicine. Zhenia went to her father.

II

The furniture was renewed. Luxury appeared in the house. The Luvers acquired a carriage and began to keep horses. The coachman was called Davletcha.

Rubber tires were quite new then. When they went for a drive everything turned and gazed after the carriage; people, gardens, churches, hens.

They did not open the door to Madame Luvers for a long time and when the carriage, out of respect for her, moved off at a slow trot, she cried after it: "Don't go far, up to the turnpike and back: be careful when you are taking the hill"; while the white sun, which reached her from the steps of the doctor's verandah, moved farther down the street and strained towards the thickset, ruddy, freckled neck of Davletcha, which it warmed and wrinkled.

They drove over the bridge. The conversation of the girders echoed roundly and cunningly and coherently, fashioned once and for all, strictly incised into the ravine and always remembered by it, in daylight and in sleep.

Vikormish,[2] clambering up the hill, tried his strength on the steep, unyielding flint; he pulled, he could do nothing and suddenly, resembling in this a creeping grasshopper, he became like a grasshopper, which is by nature made to leap and fly, unexpectedly beautiful in the humility of his unnatural efforts; it seemed that he could no longer bear to remain where he was and that he would angrily flash his wings and fly away. And so it came about. The horse pulled, flung forward his forelegs and plunged with a swift bound over the wasteland. Davletcha began to pull him up and draw on the reins. A shaggy-haired dog barked at them, mournfully and drowsily. The dust was like gunpowder. The road turned steeply to the left.

The dark street ran blindly into the red fence of a railway depot. The street was covered with strips of sunlight. The sun came slanting through the bushes and shrouded the crowd of strange figures in women's cloaks. The sun drenched them in fountains of white light which appeared to be poured from a tiptilted bucket of watery lime, and flooded the earth. The street was covered with strips of sunlight. The horse moved slowly. "Turn to the right," Zhenia ordered. "There's no road," Davletcha replied, pointing with his whip-handle at the red wall. "A blind-alley." "Then stop, I want to have a look." They were our Chinese. "I see." Davletcha, realising that his mistress was disinclined to talk with him, slowly chanted, "Whoa!" and the horse, his whole body swaying, stood as though rooted to the ground; Davletcha began to whistle softly and helpfully, compelling the horse to do what was necessary.

[2] The name usually given to horses brought up in the house (*vikormit*—to bring up). Here it is also the nickname of the horse.—*Translator's Note.*

The Chinese ran across the road, holding in their hands huge loaves of rye bread. They were in blue and resembled peasant women in trousers. Their bare heads ended in a knot over the parietal bone and seemed to have been twisted out of pocket-handkerchiefs. Several of them paused. One could distinguish them clearly. Their faces were pale, earthy, simpering. They were swarthy and filthy, like copper oxydised by poverty. Davletcha took out his tobacco pouch and began to roll a primitive cigarette. Meanwhile from the corner over there, in the direction where the Chinese were going, several women appeared. Probably they were coming for bread too. Those who were on the road began to laugh uproariously; they approached them lasciviously, waddling as though their hands were twisted with a rope behind their backs. Their curious waddling motions were emphasised by the fact that from their shoulders to their ankles they were dressed alike in a single piece of cloth, exactly in the manner of acrobats. There was nothing intimidating in them; the women did not run away, but stood there themselves laughing.

"What's the matter with you, Davletcha?" "The horse is pulling. The horse! Can't stand still! Just can't stand still!" Meanwhile Davletcha repeatedly struck Vikormish sharp blows with the reins, twitching them and then letting them hang loose. "Quietly, you'll overturn the carriage. Why do you whip him?" "I must." And only when he had entered the field and quietened the horse, which was beginning to panic, did the wily Tartar, who had borne his mistress like an arrow from the shameful scene, take the reins in his hands, seize the riding-whip and lay the to-bacco-pouch, which had remained in his hands all the time, inside the flap of his coat.

They returned by another road. Madame Luvers saw them, probably from the doctor's window. She walked to the steps at the same moment that the bridge, having

193

already told them all its fairy tale, began all over again
under the weight of the water-cart.

With the Deffendov girl, with the girl who had brought
mountain-ash into the classroom, plucked on the way to
school, Zhenia made friends at one of her examinations.
The daughter of the sacristan was taking her examination
in French after failing the first time. They made Luvers
Evgenia sit down in the first empty place. There they
made one another's acquaintance, as they sat together over
the same sentence.

Est-ce Pierre qui a volé la pomme?

Oui, c'est Pierre qui vola etc.

The fact that Zhenia had to take her lessons at home did
not put an end to the friendship between the two girls.
They continued to meet. And their meetings, owing to
her mother's opinions, were onesided: Lisa was allowed to
visit them, but for the time being Zhenia was forbidden
to go to the Deffendovs.

Their meetings, which took place at odd moments, by
snatches, did not prevent Zhenia from soon becoming
attached to her friend. She fell in love with the Deffendov
girl, that is she played an entirely passive role, becoming as
it were a barometer, watchful and inflamed with anxiety.
All Lisa's references to her classmates, who were unknown
to her, aroused in Zhenia a sensation of bitterness and
futility. Her heart sank: these were her first attacks of
jealousy. For no reason, in the strength of her anxiety,
Zhenia was convinced that Lisa was playing her false, outwardly sincere but inwardly laughing at everything in her
which was peculiar to the family of Luvers; and as soon as
she was out of sight, at home or in the classroom, she was
making merry over these things; but Zhenia considered

that it was as it should be, it was something which lay in the very nature of their attachment. These sentiments aroused by an accidental choice of an object answered the powerful demands of an instinct, which takes no cognisance of self-love and knows only to suffer and to be consumed in honour of a fetish, when it feels for the first time.

Neither Zhenia nor Lisa greatly influenced one another and Zhenia remained Zhenia, Lisa Lisa; they met and they parted—the one profoundly moved and the other emotionally undisturbed.

. . . .

The father of the Akhmedyanovs traded in iron. During the year which intervened between the birth of Nuretdin and Smagil he unexpectedly became rich. At that time Smagil began to be called Samoil, and it was decided to give the sons a Russian education. Not a single peculiarity of the free seigneurial existence was neglected by the father, but in ten years of hurried imitation, he had overshot the mark in every way. The children succeeded marvellously in following the pattern chosen by their father and the splendid range of his wilfulness remained with them, noisy and destructive, like a pair of revolving flywheels rebounding by virtue of their inertia. In the fourth class the brothers Akhmedyanov were the most genuine representatives of the fourth class mentality. They consisted of chalk broken into little pieces, cribs, gunshot, the crash of desks, obscene swear-words and red-cheeked and snub-nosed cocksureness which crackled in the frost. Seriozha made friends with them in August. By the end of September the boy had no face left. It was in the order of things. To be a typical schoolboy, and later something else as well, implied being at one with the Akhmedyanovs. And Seriozha wanted nothing so much as to be this schoolboy. Luvers placed no obstacle in the way of his son's desires. He did not notice the changes in him, but even if he had noticed them, he would have written them down to adolescence. Besides, he had other things to worry about. For some time he had suspected that he was ill and that his illness was incurable.

IV

She was not sorry for him, although everyone else was saying how disagreeable it was and how incredibly ill-timed. Negarat was too subtle even for their parents and all that was felt by the parents in relation to the foreigner was dimly conveyed to the children, as to spoilt domesticated animals. Zhenia grieved only because now nothing would be as it was before, and there remained only the three Belgians, and there would never be so much laughter as there was before.

She happened to be sitting by the table on the evening when he explained to her mother that he would have to go to Dijon for his military service. "You must be still young——" her mother said, and at once she was wracked with pity for him. But he sat down, hanging his head. The conversation flagged. "To-morrow they are coming to putty the windows," her mother said and she asked him whether she ought to close them. He said there was no need, the evening was warm and in his country the windows were not puttied even in winter. Soon her father came up to them. He too was flooded with a sense of compassion at the news. But before he began to give vent to his lamentations, he raised his eyebrows and said in a surprised voice, "To Dijon? But I thought you were a Belgian?" "Belgian, but a French subject." And Negarat began to relate the history of the emigration of his 'old people,' so amusingly that he might not have been the son of his 'old people,' so warmly that he might have been

196

reading it all from a book about foreigners. "Excuse me for interrupting," mother said. "Zhenyushka, you ought to close the window. Vika, to-morrow they will come and putty the windows. Well, go on. That uncle of yours was a fine old ruffian! Did he do it *literally* on oath?" "Yes." And he resumed his story. And he went on to discuss affairs and the papers which he had received the day before by post from the consulate; he imagined that the girl would understand nothing and was straining to understand. So he turned to her and began to explain, without showing any sign that this was his aim, to avoid hurting her pride, what this military service was. "Yes, yes. I understand. Yes. I understand. Of course I do," Zhenia repeated mechanically and gratefully.

"But why go so far? Be a soldier *here*. Learn where everyone else does," she corrected herself, imagining the meadow which rose clear on the monastery hill.

"Yes, yes. I understand. Yes, yes, yes," Zhenia repeated; but the Luvers, finding themselves at a loose end and thinking that the Belgian was filling her head with useless details, interposed their own sleepy and simplifying observations. And suddenly the moment arrived when she began to pity all those who in the old days or still more recently, were the Negarats in far-off places, men of the dispersion who set out along the unexpected road which was being thrown down from the sky, in order to become soldiers here in Ekaterinburg. So well did he explain it to her. No one had explained it to her in that way. A veil of indifference, the hypnotic veil of perception was removed from the vision of white tents: regiments faded away and transformed themselves into a group of separate individuals in military uniform, and she began to be sorry for them at the same moment that their significance brought them into life and exalted them, brought them closer to her and discoloured them.

They took their leave. "I shall leave some of my books with Tsvetkov. He is the friend I was always talking about. Please make use of them in the future, *madame*. Your son knows where I am living: he sees the landlord's family; I shall give up my room to Tsvetkov. I shall warn him beforehand."

"We'll be pleased to see him. Tsvetkov, did you say?"

"Tsvetkov."

"By all means, let him come along. We shall be delighted to meet him. When I was younger I used to know the family,"—and she looked at her husband who was standing in front of Negarat, his hands lying along the seam of his tightly-fitting coat, while he distractedly waited for a convenient opening in which to make final arrangements with the Belgian about to-morrow.

"Let him come. Only not now. I shall let him know. Yes, take it, it's yours. I haven't finished yet. I cried over it. The doctor advises me to give up reading. So as to avoid the excitement,"—and once more she looked at her husband, who hung his head, puffing and making a crackling sound with his collar, as he became more and more interested in the problem as to whether he was wearing his boots on both legs and whether they were well cleaned.

"Well now, don't forget your walking-stick. I hope we shall see one another again."

"Oh, of course. Until Friday. What day is to-day?" He was frightened, as are all those who go away in similar circumstances.

"Wednesday. Vika, Wednesday? Vika, Wednesday? Wednesday *Ecoutez*." Father's turn came at last: "*Demain*——" and both walked down the stairs.

·   ·   ·   ·   ·

V

They walked and talked, and on innumerable occasions
she fell into a gentle sprint so as to avoid lagging behind
Seriozha and in order to keep pace with him. They walked
very quickly and her coat fidgeted on her, because she
rowed with her arms to help her move forward, but kept
her hands in her pockets. It was cold. Under her goloshes
the thin ice burst musically. They were going on an errand
for her mother to buy a present for the departing guest,
and they were talking.

"So they were taking him to the station?"

"Yes."

"But why did he sit in the straw?"

"What do you mean?"

"In the cart. All of him, from the feet up. People don't
sit like that."

"I've already told you. It's because he's a prisoner—a
criminal."

"Are they going to take him to prison?"

"No, to Perm. We haven't got a prison. Look where
you're going."

Their way led them across the road and past the coppersmith's shop. During the whole of the summer the doors
stood wide open, and Zhenia used to associate the crossroad with the peculiar friendly warmth which the open
jaws of the workshop imparted to it. All through July,
August and September carts would pull up, blocking the
exits; peasants, mostly Tartars, would congregate in crowds;
pails would roll on the ground and pieces of gutter-piping,
broken and rusted; and it was there, rather than anywhere
else, that the blazing dense sun transformed the crowd
into a gypsy encampment and painted the Tartars in
gypsy colours and sank in the terrible dust at the hour

when they slaughtered the chickens behind the neighbouring wattle-fence; and there the limbers, disengaged from under the carts, were plunged by the shafts into the dust with the rubbed palate-plates of the coupling-bolts.

Pails and scrap iron lay in confusion and were now powdered with a faint frost. But the doors were shut tight, as though it was a holiday, against the cold, and the crossroad was deserted; but through the circular venthole there came a smell which Zhenia recognised, the smell of musty firedamp which broke into a clattering scream and striking the nostrils precipitated on the palate an inexpensive and effervescing fizzy drink.

"And is the prison in Perm?"

"Yes. The central offices. I think it is better to go this way. Nearer. It's in Perm, because that's the administrative town, while Ekaterinburg is only a provincial town. Very small."

The road in front of the private houses was faced with red brick and lined with bushes. On the road lay traces of the weak, lustreless sun. Seriozha endeavoured to walk as noisily as possible.

"If you tickle barberry in spring, when it flowers, with a pin, it quickly flutters its leaves as though it was alive."

"I know."

"And you are afraid of being tickled?"

"Yes."

"That means your nerves are bad. The Akhmedyanovs say that anyone who is afraid of being tickled . . ."

And they went on, Zhenia running, Seriozha walking with unnatural strides; and her coat fidgeted on her. They saw Dikikh at the very moment when the wicket-gate, which revolved like a turnstile on a shaft, barred their way and prevented them from going on. They saw him in the distance: he was coming out of the shop they were going into, separated from them by half the length of a block.

Dikikh was not alone; behind him there walked a slight man who seemed to be trying to hide the fact that he was limping. It occurred to Zhenia that she had already seen him somewhere. They passed, without greeting one another. They turned away obliquely. Dikikh did not notice the children; he wore thigh-boots and often raised his hands with outspread fingers. He did not acquiesce and with all ten of them demonstrated that his companion . . . (But where had she seen him? A long time ago. But where? It must have been in Perm, in her childhood.)

"Stop!" Something was annoying Seriozha. He dropped to one knee. "Wait a moment."

"Did it hook?"

"Yes, it did. Such idiots, they can't beat a nail in properly."

"Have you got it?"

"Wait a moment, I can't think where. I know that man limping. Thank goodness!"

"Torn it?"

"No, it's all right, thank Heaven. That tear in the lining is an old one. It's not my fault. Come on. Wait a moment. I'm only brushing my knee. Now it's all right. Come on."

"I know him. He comes from the Akhmedyanovs' house. He is Negarat's friend. Don't you remember? I spoke about him. He brings some people together and they drink all night and there is a light in their window. Don't you remember when I spent a night with the Akhmedyanovs? On the birthday of Samoil. Well, doesn't that help? Now do you remember?"

She remembered. She realised she had made a mistake. In this case it was impossible to have seen the limping man in Perm, as she had at first imagined. But she continued to feel otherwise, and in her reticence with regard to these sensations, while sifting among her memories of

201

Perm, she followed her brother in performing certain movements: she took hold of something, she overstepped something and looking around her, found herself in the half-light of counters, among shelves and packing-cases and fastidious greetings and servile attention . . . and . . . Seriozha was talking.

The name, which he wanted, of the bookseller who dealt in all kinds of tobacco, did not appear; but he put them at their ease and assured him that the promised Turgeniev had been sent from Moscow and was now on its way, and he had only just this moment—a moment ago—spoken about this same book with Mr. Tsvetkov, their tutor. His shiftiness and his error with regard to Tsvetkov amused the children; they took leave of him and went home with empty hands.

As they were leaving Zhenia turned to her brother with the question:

"Seriozha, I always forget! Do you know the street which can be seen from our wood-piles?"

"No, I have never been there before."

"Not true. I saw you myself."

"On the wood-pile? You . . . ?"

"I'm not talking about the wood-pile, but the street behind the Cherep-Savvich's garden."

"Oh, that! Of course! Straight ahead. Behind the garden, right along. There are sheds and firewood. Wait a moment. You mean our courtyard? That courtyard? Ours! How clever! Whenever I went there I used to think how nice it would be to go as far as the wood-piles, and then from the wood-piles to the attic. There is a ladder there— I've seen it. Are you sure it is really our courtyard?"

"Seriozha, will you show me the road there?"

"Again? But the courtyard is ours. What is there to show? You yourself . . ."

"Seriozha, you still don't understand. I'm talking about

the road and you're talking about the courtyard. I'm talking about the road. Show me the way to the road. Show
me how to get there. Show me, Seriozha."

"But I don't understand. We went there to-day . . . and
we're going there again soon."

"Really?"

"Yes. And the coppersmith? . . . At the corner."

"Then the one covered in dust . . ."

"Is the very one you are talking about. While the
Cherep-Savvich's is at the end, on the right. Don't stand
still or you'll be late for dinner. It's lobster to-day."

They spoke about something else. The Akhmedyanovs
had promised to teach him how to tin a samovar. This led
them to the question of solder, and he told her that it
was a kind of ore which resembled pewter, and with it they
solder tin boxes and make cauldrons. This tin was soldered
on to it, and the pots were heated, and the Akhmedyanovs
knew all about this.

They had to run, otherwise a line of carts would have
held them back. And they forgot—she her request about
the unfrequented sidestreet, and he his promise to show
her where it was. They passed close to the shop door, and
it was there, while they were inhaling the warm, greasy
smoke which derived from the scourings of copper candle-
sticks and copper mountings, that Zhenia suddenly remembered where she had seen the limping man and the three
strangers, and what they were doing, and a moment later
she realised that it was Tsvetkov, the man the bookseller
had been talking about, who was the limping man.

VI

Negarat left in the evening. Father went to see him off.
He returned late at night from the station. His appearance
at the porter's lodge aroused an immense and not quickly

203

appeased state of alarm. They came out with lanterns, they called out. Rain fell and the geese, which had been let loose, cackled.

The morning was cloudy and shaky. The moist grey street bounded like indiarubber, the foul rain quivered and splashed up mud; carriages sprang up and down and scattered mud on men in goloshes as they crossed the street.

Zhenia returned home. Echoes of the uproar at night were still being heard in the courtyard in the morning. They refused to allow her to go in the carriage. She walked towards her friend's house, after saying that she was going out to buy hempseed. But when she had gone halfway, she was sure she would not find the road from the shopping district to the Deffendovs, and turned back. And then she remembered that it was too early and in any case Lisa would be at school. She was wet through and trembling. The wind lifted. But still it did not clear up. A cold white light flew along the road and like a leaf stuck to the soggy flagstones. Muddy clouds hurried away from the town, hustling giddily, in a state of panic agitation, at the end of the square, beyond the three-branched street-lamps.

The man who was changing his house was either very slovenly or unprincipled. The furniture of his poorly furnished study was not loaded on to the lorry, but simply placed in it exactly as it had been placed in the room, and the casters of the armchairs, seen under the white dust-covers, slid along the boards, as on a parquet floor, with every quiver of the vehicle. The dust-covers were as white as snow, although they were drenched through. They caught one's eye so sharply that on looking at them everything else assumed the same colour: the cobblestones gnawed by the bad weather, the freezing water in the ditches under the walls, the birds flying away from the stables, the trees flying after them, pieces of lead and even the fig tree in the tub which trembled, awkwardly bowing its greetings from the cart at everything which flew past.

The cart-load was absurd. Involuntarily it directed attention to itself. A peasant walked alongside and the lorry, lurching broadly, moved at a walking pace and knocked against the posts set up on the road. Above it, in croaking tatters, floated the drenched and leaden word: t-o-w-n, giving birth inside the girl's head to a multitude of ideas as fugitive as the cold October light which was flying over the road and falling into the water.

"He will catch cold when he unpacks his things," she thought, at the sight of their unknown owner. And she imagined a man—*just a man walking falteringly, with uneven gait*, propping up his goods and chattels in the different corners of his new house. She was quick to imagine his movements and mannerisms, especially how he would pick up a rag, hobble round the tub and begin to wipe away the clouded sediment of frost which lay on the leaves of the fig tree. And then he would catch cold, shiver and develop a temperature. Sure to catch cold. Zhenia imagined this very vividly. Very vividly. The cart rumbled down the hill towards Isset. Zhenia had to turn left.

.   .   .   .   .

It derived probably from someone's heavy footsteps behind the door. The tea in the glass, on the table, by the bed, rose and fell. A slice of lemon in the tea rose and fell. The sunny stripes on the wallpaper were swaying. They were swaying in pillars like the bottles full of syrup which stand in the shops behind signboards, on which a Turk is smoking a pipe.

On which a Turk . . . is smoking . . . a pipe. Smoking . . . a pipe.

It derived probably from someone's footsteps. The patient went to sleep again.

205

Zhenia fell ill the day after Negarat's departure; on the very day when she learned after a stroll that Aksinya had given birth to a boy during the night, on the very day when, at the sight of the lorry-load of furniture, she decided that rheumatism lay in wait for the owner. For a fortnight, she lay in a fever, thickly spattered over the sweat with painful red pepper which burnt and clung to her eyelids and the corners of her lips. Perspiration worried her and a sensation of monstrous obesity mingled with the feeling of being stung. As though the flame which made her swell was being poured into her by a summer wasp. As though its sting, as thin as a grey hair, remained in her while she longed to take it out, more than once and in more than one way. Now from the purple cheekbone, now from the inflamed shoulder aching under her chemise, now from somewhere else. Meanwhile she was convalescing. The feeling of weakness was manifest everywhere.

This feeling of weakness gave way, at its own risk and peril, to a strange geometry of its own, provoking a slight giddiness and a sensation of nausea.

Having begun, for example, with some episode on the counterpane, this feeling of weakness began to construct upon it rows of gradually increasing blank spaces, which quickly became an immense void, as the twilight tended to assume the shape of the square which lay at the basis of this maniac play with space. Or else, separating from the pattern of the wallpaper, stripe by stripe, it drove the widths before the girl as smoothly as oil, substituting one for another and also, as in all these sensations, harassing her with a regular and gradual growth in the dimensions. Or else it tormented the sick child with depths which went on without end, betraying from the very beginning, from its first trick on the parquet floor, its own fathomlessness, allowing the bed to fall silently into the depths, silently;

and with the bed went the girl. Her head was like a
lump of sugar thrown into the abyss of an insipid and
menacingly empty chaos, and it dissolved and disappeared
in it.

It derived from the heightened sensitivity of the laby-
rinths of her ears.

It derived from someone's footsteps. The lemon rose
and fell. The sunlight rose and fell on the wallpaper. At
last she woke up. Her mother came in, congratulated her
on her recovery and produced on the girl the impression
of someone reading strange thoughts. While waking up,
she had already heard something similar. These were the
congratulations of her own hands, feet, elbows, knees; and
she accepted them, as she stretched herself. Their greetings even woke her up. And there was her mother as well.
The coincidence was strange.

The household came in and went out, sat down and
stood up. She asked questions and received answers. Some
things were changed during her illness, others were left
unchanged. These she did not touch, those she did not
leave in peace. Her mother was clearly unchanged. Obviously her father had not changed. The things which had
changed were: she herself, Seriozha, the diffusion of light
in the room, the silence of the others, and still something
more? Had there been a fall of snow? No, it fell a little,
melted, froze, impossible to decide which, bare, without
snow. She hardly noticed whom she was questioning and
what she was talking about. Replies came hurriedly one
after the other. Healthy people came and went. Lisa came
in. They were arguing. Then they remembered that
measles does not come twice, and they let her in. Dikikh
visited her. She hardly noticed what replies came from
whom. When they had all left for dinner and she was
alone with Ulyasha, she thought of how they had laughed
over her stupid questions in the kitchen. Now she took

care not to ask such questions. She would ask sensible practical questions in the voice of someone who is grown up. She asked whether Aksinya had been pregnant again. The maid tinkled with a small spoon, removed the glass and turned away. "Darling, give her a rest now. She can't always be pregnant, Zhenichka . . ." And she ran away, forgetting to close the door and the whole kitchen roared as though the shelves of china had crashed down, and the laughter became a howl, and it passed through the hands of the charwoman and Halim, and blazed underneath their hands and clattered swiftly and fervently, as though they were beginning to fight after a quarrel, but at that moment someone came up and closed the forgotten door.

She should not have asked about this. It was still more stupid.

VII

Will it thaw again? It would mean that they could go for a drive to-day: it was still impossible to harness the sleigh. With a cold nose and shivering hands Zhenia stood for hours by the little window. Dikikh had gone a short while before. Previously he had been displeased with her. How can one learn when the birds are singing outside and the sky drones, but when the droning dies down, the cocks begin to crow again? The clouds were ragged and mudstained, like the bald rugs you wrap round your knees. The day butted the windowpane with its snout, like a calf in its steaming stall. Is it not spring? But as by a hoop, the air after lunch is intercepted by the dove-coloured frost, the sky grows hollow and fades away; the clouds breathe audibly with a whistling sound; and flowing towards the wintry darkness of the north, the fleeting hours tear the last leaves from the trees, shear the lawns, break through the crevices, cut through the breast. The muzzles of northern storms grow black behind the houses: they point to the courtyard charged with the immensity of November.

But it is still only October. No one remembers such a winter. They say the winter crops have perished, they are afraid of starving. As though someone was waving and encircling with a wand gutter-piping and roofs and hen-coops. Over there will be smoke, there—snow, here—rime. But so far neither. The deserted, hollow-cheeked twilight yearns for them. They strain their eyes and the earth aches with the early lamplight and the fires in the houses, just as the head aches during long anticipation on account of the fixedness of the eyes. Everything is strained and expectant; the firewood is already stacked in the kitchen, and for a fortnight the clouds have been saturated with snow, the air is pregnant with darkness. But when will the magician, who has already enclosed everything the eye sees within magic circles, utter an incantation and conjure up the winter, whose spirit is already at the doors?

And yet, how they neglected it! Certainly no one paid any attention to the calendar in the schoolroom. They tore off the leaves of their calendar. But still! The twenty-ninth of August! Gosh! as Seriozha would have said. A red-letter day. Decollation of St. John the Baptist. It was easy to lift it from the nails. Having nothing better to do, she amused herself by tearing up the leaves. She made these movements in a spirit of boredom and quickly ceased to understand what she was doing, but from time to time she repeated to herself: thirtieth; to-morrow—thirty-first.

"This is the third day she hasn't been out of the house!" These words, resounding from the corridor, aroused her from her reverie, and she realised how far she had entered into the work she was doing. She had passed the Annunciation. Her mother touched her hands. "Say please, Zhenia . . ."—the rest of the sentence vanished into the distance, as though unspoken. Interrupting her mother, as though in a dream, Zhenia asked Madame Luvers to say, "Decollation of John the Baptist." Her mother repeated the words, perplexed. She did not say, "Decallation." This is what Aksinya said.

The next moment Zhenia was seized with amazement at what she had done. What was it? What had made her do it? What had put it into her head? Was it she, Zhenia, who had asked this? Or could she really have thought that her mother would . . . ? How fantastic and improbable: Who had invented all this?

Her mother was still standing there. She did not believe her ears. She looked at her daughter with wide-open eyes. This prank made her uneasy. The question was like a mockery: meanwhile tears stood in the girl's eyes.

.   .   .   .   .

Her dim forebodings came true. While they were driving, she heard clearly how the air was becoming silky, the clouds pulpy and the ring of the horses' hooves was growing tenuous. They had not yet lit the fires when dry, grey flakes began to twirl and roam freely in the air. As soon as they passed the bridge, the separate snowflakes disappeared and the snow began to fall in a solid coagulating mass. Davletcha slid down from the coachbox and lifted the leather roof. For Zhenia and Seriozha it became dark and close. She wanted to rage like the foul weather which was raging all round her. They knew that Davletcha was taking them home, because once more they heard the bridge under Vikormish's hooves. The streets were unrecognisable: there were simply no streets. Night came down a moment later and the town, panic-stricken, moved countless thousands of thick, pale lips. Seriozha leaned out, and resting on his elbow, gave orders that they should drive to the industrial school. Zhenia was growing exhausted with excitement as she recognised all the secrets and delights of winter from the manner in which Seriozha's words resounded in the air. Davletcha shouted in reply that they had to return home so as not to tire the horses, the master and mistress were going to the theatre and would have to drive by sleigh. Zhenia remembered that her parents would be going out and they would be left alone. She decided to stay up late at night comfortably, with a lamp and a copy of the tales of *Kot-Murlika*, which is not for children. She would have to get it from her mother's bedroom. And chocolate. And read, sucking chocolate and listening to the wind sweeping down the street.

The snowstorm was increasing. The sky quivered and white kingdoms and countries toppled from the sky, impossible to keep score of them, mysterious and terrible. It was obvious that these territories, falling from no one knew where, had never heard about life and the earth; arctic and blind, they covered the earth, neither seeing it nor knowing anything about it.

They were exquisitely terrifying, these kingdoms; ravishingly satanic. Zhenia revelled as she looked at them. The air reeled, seizing at whatever fell in the distance, with immense labour, the fields shuddered as though they had been struck with lashes. Everything became confused. Night rushed upon them, a fierce night of ignobly churning grey hair which cut and blinded. Everything drove apart, with a scream, disregarding the road. A shout and an echo disappeared, without meeting; a confusion of sounds borne upwards to various roofs. Snowstorm.

They stamped for a long time in the hall, shaking the snow from their swollen white sheepskin coats. How much water flowed from their goloshes on to the chequered linoleum! Many egg-shells were scattered on the table and the pepper-pot, extracted from the cruet, had not been put in its place, and pepper was strewn all over the table-cloth, on the flowing yolks and the tin of unfinished sardines. Their parents had already finished supper, but they were still sitting in the dining-room, hurrying their slow children. They did not blame them; they had taken supper earlier because they were going to the theatre. Mother could not make up her mind. She did not know whether to go or not, and sat there in melancholy state. Looking at her, Zhenia remembered that, strictly speaking, she herself could not be said to be happy—at last she managed to unclasp the malignant hook—but on the contrary she was rather melancholy; and going into the dining-room, she asked where they had taken the hazel-nut tart. Father looked at mother and said no one was compelling them to go and they had better stay at home. "But we're going," mother said. "We must have a change and the doctor has allowed it. We must make up our minds." "But where's the tart?" Zhenia asked again, and she heard the reply that tarts don't run away, that one has also to eat what comes before a tart, that one does not begin with tarts and it was in the cupboard—as if she had come here for the first time in her life and did not know their usual ways—so her father said; and again turning to her mother, he repeated, "We must make up our minds." "It's decided, we go," and mournfully smiling at Zhenia, her mother went away to dress. But Seriozha, rapping his spoon on the egg and looking closely, because he was afraid of missing it, with a business-like air, as though preoccupied, warned his father that the weather had changed—a snowstorm, and he should bear this in mind, and he began to laugh: from his dripping nose something inelegant appeared, he began to fidget and took his handkerchief from the pocket of his tight, formal trousers, then blew his nose, as his father had taught him, "without endangering the eardrums." He took up his spoon and looked straight at his father, ruddy and washed clean by the drive, and said: "On our way out we saw the friend of Negarat. Do you know him?" "Evans?" his father asked distractedly. "We don't know that man," Zhenia retorted hotly. "Vika!" a voice sounded from the bedroom. Father got up and went to the voice. In the doorway Zhenia collided with Ulyasha who was bringing in the burning lamp. Soon an adjoining door banged. It was Seriozha going to his room. He had surpassed himself during the day: his sister loved the idea that the friend of the Akhmedyanovs should act like a boy, when it was possible to say of him that he was in his school uniform.

The doors swung. They stamped out in gumboots. At last they had gone. The letter said: "Up to now she hadn't been selfish and if they wanted anything, they should ask her as before," but when the "dear sister," overladen with greetings and kind regards, began to distribute them among her numerous relations, Ulyasha, becoming for once Juliana, thanked her mistress, turned down the lamp and went away, bearing the letter, a small bottle of ink and what remained of the greasy paper.

Zhenia returned to the problem. She did not confine the repeating decimals between brackets. She continued the division, writing down one set of numbers after another. She could not forsee the end. The repeating decimals in the quotient grew and grew. "What if measles returns?" flashed through her mind. "To-day Dikikh said something about infinity." She ceased to understand what she was doing. She felt that similar things had already happened to her earlier in the day, and also she wanted to sleep or cry, but she could not think what it was and what it was called, because it was not in her power to think carefully. The noise outside the window died away. The snowstorm was gradually dying down. Decimals were completely new to her. There was not sufficient margin on

the right. Se decided to begin again and write more carefully, checking each link. It was very quiet in the street.
She was afraid of forgetting the number she had taken
down from the next figure, and of not being able to retain
the product in her head. The window won't run away, she
thought, continuing to pour threes and sevens into the
fathomless quotient,—but I shall hear them in time;
silence all round; they won't come up quickly; in fur
coats, and her mother with child; but the important thing
is that 3773 keeps on recurring; one can simply write it
down or cancel it out. Suddenly she remembered that
Dikikh had actually told her earlier in the day, "You
mustn't keep them but simply throw them away." She got
up and went to the window.

It grew light outside. Rare snowflakes came sailing out
of the dark night. They swarmed towards the street-lamp,
swam round it, wriggled and fell out of sight. Others
swam up and took their places. The street glittered, paved
with a carpet of snow which promised good sleighing. It
was white; it glistened; it was sweet, like gingerbread in
the fables. Zhenia stood by the window, looking at the
rugs and the figures which the Hans Andersen sheen of the
snowflakes produced on the lamp-post. She stood there
for a while and then went into her mother's room for the
tales of Kot-Murlika. She went in without a light. It
was possible to see. The roof of the shed poured into the
room a white moving sheen. The beds froze under the
moans of the huge roof and they shone resplendently.
Here in disorder lay scattered moiré silks. The tiny blouses
gave off an oppressive scent of calico and armpits. The
cupboard smelt of violet, blue-black, like the night outside, like the warm and arid darkness in which all these
frozen particles moved. One of the metal globes on the
bed gleamed like a single bead. The other was extinguished
because a shirt had been thrown over it. Zhenia screwed

up her eyes, the bead moved away from the floor and swam towards the wardrobe. Zhenia remembered why she had come. With the book in her hands she walked towards one of the windows of the bedroom. The night was starry. Winter had arrived in Ekaterinburg. She glanced at the courtyard and began to think of Pushkin. She decided to ask her tutor to make her write a composition about Onyegin.

Seriozha wanted to talk. He said: "Have you scented yourself? Give me some." All day he had been very nice to her. Very ruddy in the face. She thought there would never be another evening like this. She wanted to be alone.

Zhenia withdrew into her room and took up the book of tales. She read one story and began another, holding her breath. She was absorbed in it and did not hear her brother going to bed on the other side of the wall. A strange game took possession of her face. She was not conscious of it. Now her face spread like a fish's; her lips parted and her death-pale pupils, rooted to the page with terror, refused to rise, afraid of finding *this thing* behind the wardrobe. Now her head began to nod in sympathy with the print, as though it was applauding her, like a head which admired someone's behaviour and rejoiced in the turn of affairs. She read slowly when she came to the description of the lakes and plunged headlong into the dregs of a scene at night with a lump of scorched Bengal fire, on which the illumination depended. At one place the hero lost his way and cried out intermittently, listening for an answer and hearing only the echo of his own voice. Zhenia had to clear her throat because of the inaudible gutteral cry which stood there. The name "Wyra"—not a Russian name— helped her out of her stupor. She laid the book aside and began to think. "So this is what winter is like in Asia. What are the Chinese doing on a dark night like this?" Zhenia's eyes fell on the clock. "Really it must be terrifying to be with the Chinese in the darkness." Once more she looked at the clock and became frightened. At any moment her parents might appear. It was already twelve o'clock. She unlaced her boots and remembered that she had to put the book back in its place.

.   .   .   .   .

Zhenia jumped up. She sat up on the bed, staring straight in front of her. It was not a thief, there are many of them and they stamp their feet and talk loudly, as in the daytime. Suddenly a piercing cry broke out, and they shuffled something forward, overturning the chairs. It was a woman's cry. Zhenia gradually recognised them all; everyone except the woman. An incredible scamper of feet broke out. Doors began to bang. When one of the more distant doors started banging, it was as though they were choking the woman. But it swung open again and the sound scalded the house with a burning, welting scream. Zhenia's hair stood on end: the woman was her mother, she *realised*. Ulyasha was wailing, and after once hearing her father's voice, she did not hear it any more. They were pushing Seriozha somewhere and he was shouting, "Don't dare to lock the door!" whereupon Zhenia, barefooted, wearing only her nightshirt, rushed into the corridor. Her father nearly knocked her over. He was still in his overcoat, and as he ran he was shouting something to Ulyasha. "Papa!" She saw him running out of the bathroom with a white jug. "Papa." "Where's Lisa?" he shouted as he ran, in a voice which was not his own. Splashing water over the floor, he disappeared behind the door, and when, a moment later, he appeared in shirt-sleeves and without a waistcoat, Zhenia found herself in Ulyasha's arms, and she did not hear the words which were spoken despairingly in a deep, heart-rending whisper.

"What is the matter with mother?" Instead of replying, Ulyasha repeated over and over again in one breath,

"Don't, don't, Zhenitchka darling, go to sleep, sleep, rest, lie on your side—ah-ah, my God!—darling!" "Don't, don't," she repeated, sheltering her as though she was a child, trying to move away; don't, don't, but why don't— she did not speak and her face was wet and her hair tousled. In the third door behind her a lock clicked.

Zhenia lit a match to see how long it would be before dawn. It was exactly one o'clock. She was startled. Had she slept for less than an hour? But the noise had not died down there in her parents' room. Groaning broke out, hatched out, shot out. It was followed a moment later by a limitless, ageless silence. Hurried footsteps broke into it, and frequent guarded conversations. Then a bell rang. Then another. Followed by words, quarrels, orders—there were so many that it was almost as though the rooms were blazing with voices, like tables set under a thousand dying candelabras.

Zhenia fell asleep. She slept with tears in her eyes. She dreamed there were guests. She counted them and always miscalculated. Always there was one too many. And whenever she discovered that she had made a mistake, she was as panic-stricken as when she realised that it was not just anyone, but her mother.

.   .   .   .   .

How could one not rejoice at the clear, sunlit morning. Seriozha thought of games in the courtyard, snowballs, mock battles with the neighbouring children. They served tea in the classroom. They told them—the floor-polishers were in the dining-room. Their father entered. At once it was obvious that he knew nothing about the floor-polishers. Their father told them the true cause of the changes which had been made. Their mother was ill. Silence was required. Ravens flew over the white-shrouded street with wide, croaking cries. A small sledge ran past, led by a small mare. She was not yet accustomed to her new snaffle and dragged

217

her paces. "You're going to the Deffendovs, I have already arranged it. And you . . ." "Why?" Zhenia interrupted him. But Seriozha guessed why and anticipated his father. "So as not to catch the infection," he explained to his sister. The street gave him no peace. He ran up to the little window, as though they were beckoning him from there. The Tartar, walking along in his new clothes, was as spruce and handsome as a pheasant. He wore a sheepskin cap. His uncovered sheepskin glowed more warmly than leather. He walked with a waddling movement, swinging his body because the crimson ornament of his boot stood in no relation to the construction of a human foot; for the design broke apart, paying little attention to whether they were legs or teacups or tiles from the roof of the porch. But most remarkable of all—meanwhile the groans which were being uttered weakly in the bedroom increased, and his father went into the corridor, forbidding them to follow—but most remarkable of all were the clear traces he drew with the clean and narrow toes of his boots on the smooth field. Against these sculptured and orderly rows, the snow seemed whiter, more satiny. "Here's a letter. You'll give it to the Deffendovs. Himself? Understand? Well, get ready. They'll bring you all here. Go down by the back stairs. The Akhmedyanovs are waiting for you."

"Are they really?" the son asked ironically.

"Yes, you will dress in the kitchen." He spoke absentmindedly, and without hurrying, led them into the kitchen where their sheepskin coats, hats and mittens lay in a huge heap on a stool. From the stairs came a rush of winter air. Aiyok, the frozen cry of the passing sleighs remained in the air. They were in a hurry and could not get their arms in the sleeves. There came from their clothes the scent of cupboards and sleepy furs. "What are you fussing about?" "Don't put it on the edge. It will fall over. What is the news?" "She's still groaning," the maid gathered up her apron and bent down, throwing some logs under the flames of the chattering kitchen range. "It's not my work," she complained indignantly, and went off on her round of the rooms. A battered black pail contained scattered pieces of broken glass and yellow prescriptions. The towels were impregnated with dishevelled and crumpled blood. The towels shone. They wanted to be trodden down, like smouldering flames. Blank water was boiling in the saucepans. All round stood white beakers and wonderfully shaped mortars, as in a chemist's shop. In the shadows the small Halim was chopping up ice. "Was there much left over from the summer?" Seriozha asked. "There'll soon be the new ice." Give me some. You're not breaking it up properly." "Why not properly? I must break it up. For the bottles."

"Well, are you ready?"

But Zhenia was still running about the house. Seriozha went to the stairs, and while he was waiting for his sister, he began to drum with a log on the iron banisters.

VIII

At the Deffendovs they sat down to supper. The grandmother, making the sign of the cross, fell back into her armchair. The lamp glowed dully and smoked: at one moment they were turning the screw too tightly, at another, they left it too loose. The dry hand of Deffendov often stretched towards the screw, and when he slowly let himself fall into his chair, as he withdrew his hand from the lamp, his hands were shaking with a vibrating movement, not at all the movement of an old man—as though he was lifting a wineglass filled to the brim. The ends of his fingers trembled at the fingernails.

He spoke in a clear, level voice, as though he formed his conversation not with sounds, but composed his words

219

from the alphabet, and he pronounced everything, including the accents.

The swollen neck of the lamp was on fire, surrounded by tendrils of geranium and heliotrope. Cockroaches came to warm themselves against the warm glass and the hour hands advanced. Time crept as in winter. Time festered. In the courtyard it became numb, putrid. Below the window it scurried, tripped along, doubling and trebling in will-o-the-wisps.

Deffendova placed some liver on the table. The dish steamed, seasoned with onions. Deffendov said something, often repeating the words: "I recommend . . ." and Lisa cackled uninterruptedly, but Zhenia did not hear them. Since the day before she had wanted to cry. Now she thirsted after tears. There in her short coat, which had been made according to her mother's instructions.

Deffendov understood what was the matter with her. He tried to amuse her. But he began to talk to her as he would talk to a small child; soon afterwards he came to grief at the opposite extreme. His joking questions frightened and confused her. He groped blindly into the soul of his daughter's young friend, as though he was asking of her heart how old it was. He conceived this plan after *faultlessly* detecting one of Zhenia's characteristics, of playing upon the one he had noticed and of helping the child to forget about her home: and in doing this, he reminded her that she was among strangers.

Suddenly she broke down. She stood up, childishly confused, and she muttered, "Thank you very much. I have eaten enough—really. Could I look at the pictures?" And blushing darkly at the sight of their general perplexity, she added, nodding her head towards an adjacent room, "Walter Scott? Could I?"

"Go away, my dear. Go away," the grandmother murmured, riveting Lisa to her chair with her eyebrows. "The poor child—" she turned to her son, when the two halves of the claret-coloured curtain closed behind Zhenia.

The grim series of magazines weighed down the bookshelves and underneath them glowed the faint gold of a complete series of Karamzin. A rose-coloured lamp descended from the ceiling, forsaking a pair of shabby armchairs. The small carpet, merging into complete darkness, surprised her feet.

Zhenia imagined herself going in, sitting down and bursting into tears. Tears started from her eyes, but grief did not break through. How to pull aside this loneliness which weighed down upon her from the previous day like a beam? Tears possessed no power over it: they could not lift the beam. To help them, she began to think of her mother.

For the first time in her life, preparing to sleep among strangers, she measured the depth of her attachment to this precious person, the dearest in the world.

Suddenly she heard Lisa laughing behind the curtain. "Ekh, what a fidget, what a devil you are!" the old grandmother coughed up, swaying from side to side. Zhenia was surprised at the thought that she once imagined she loved this girl whose laughter resounded so close to her, at once so far away and so unnecessary. And something in her turned over, giving her the strength to cry at the same moment that her mother entered fully into her consciousness: her mother still suffering, still surrounded by the events of the previous day, like someone remaining on the platform, among the crowd which had come to see people off, while the train of time bore Zhenia away.

But really it was this penetrating glance, which was utterly unbearable—this glance which Madame Luvers bestowed on her yesterday in the classroom. It carved a way into her memory and refused to leave. Everything Zhenia now suffered lay concentrated in this glance. As though it was something which ought to be taken, something precious which they had forgotten and considered negligible.

One might lose one's senses at this thought, so tumultuous was its drunken and mischievous bitterness, and its everlastingness. Zhenia stood by the window and cried noiselessly; tears flowed and she did not wipe them away; her hands were working, although she was holding nothing. Her hands were held erect, violently, vigorously and obstinately.

A sudden thought occurred to her. She suddenly felt that she was terribly like her mother. This feeling was combined with a sensation of vivid certainty, sufficiently powerful to contrive that the idea should become reality, if it was not already reality, and make her similar to her mother only by the force of a sweetly obliterating state of mind. This feeling entered into her so sharply that she began to groan. *It was the feeling of a woman perceiving from within herself, inwardly, her outward charm.* Zhenia herself could not render an account of what had happened. She felt this for the first time. In one thing only she was not mistaken. Thus agitated, turning away from her daughter and the governess, Madame Luvers once stood by the window and bit her lip, beating her lorgnette against her gloved palm.

She went back to the Deffendovs, drunk with tears and transfigured; she walked, not in her own way, but in a changed way, wide, dreamily-disjointed and new. As he saw her coming, Deffendov realised that the conception he had formed of the girl during her absence was in no way justified. He would attempt to make a new one the moment he was not disturbed by the samovar.

Deffendova, going into the kitchen for a tray, laid the samovar on the floor and all their glances were concentrated on the gleaming copper, as though it were alive, possessing a mischievous waywardness which vanished the moment they placed it on the table. Zhenia took her place. She decided to enter into conversation with all of them. Vaguely she felt that the choice of the conversation now lay with her. Or else they would maintain her in her former isolation, not noticing that her mother was there, with her and in herself. And this shortsightedness on their part would be painful to her, but still more painful to her mother. As though encouraged by this last idea—"Vassa Vasilievna"—she turned to Deffendova, who was with immense difficulty drawing the samovar to the edge of the tray.

.   .   .   .   .

"Could you have a child?" Lisa did not immediately reply to Zhenia. "Sch, not so loud, don't raise your voice so. Well, of course, like every other girl." She spoke in intermittent whispers. Zhenia did not see the face of her friend. Lisa searched on the table for a match, but did not find one.

She knew much more about it than Zhenia; she knew *everything*; as children know things, learning from strange words. In such cases those natures which are particularly beloved by their Creator revolt, stir up rebellion and turn wild. One cannot go through this experience without exhibiting pathological phenomena. It would be contrary to nature: childish madness at this age is only the seal of a deep normality.

Once in a corner, Lisa was told in a whisper about different terrors and uglinesses. She did not choke at what she had heard, but bore everything in her brain along the street and brought it with her to the house. On the way she lost nothing of what was said to her and she took care to preserve all the foulness. She knew everything. Her organism did not burst into flame, her heart did not begin to beat alarm and her soul did not strike blows on her mind, because it dared to recognise something apart from her, not

223

from her own lips, without asking her permission.

"I know." ("You don't know anything," Lisa was thinking.) "I know," Zhenia repeated. "I'm not talking about that, but this—don't you feel that you . . . well . . . walk a step and suddenly bear a child and well—" "Do come in," Lisa replied hoarsely, overcoming her laughter. "You've certainly found a place to shout in. They'll hear you outside."

The conversation took place in Lisa's room. Lisa spoke so quietly that they could hear the water dripping from the basin. She had already found the matches, but she was slow in lighting them, incapable of giving a serious expression to her dancing cheeks. She did not want to hurt her friend. She spared the girl's ignorance, because she did not know that one could speak of these things otherwise than by means of expressions which could not be mentioned here, at home, before an acquaintance who was not going to school. She lit the lamp. Luckily the pail was full to overflowing, and Lisa hurriedly wiped the floor, concealing a new fit of laughter in her apron and in smacking the cloth, until at last she broke out into open laughter, having at last discovered a real excuse. She had dropped her comb into the pail.

.   .   .   .   .

During these days she did nothing except think of her family and wait for the hour when they would come to fetch her. During the day, after Lisa had gone to school and the old grandmother remained alone in the house, Zhenia dressed and walked by herself in the street.

Life in the suburb bore little resemblance to life in the places where the Luvers were accustomed to live. For the greater part of the day here life was empty and boring. There was nothing for the eye to revel in. It encountered nothing which was not fit to become either a rod or a broom. The coal was lolling. The blackened dish-water was poured into the street, and at once became white, having turned into ice. At certain hours the streets were full of ordinary people. Workmen crawled in the snow like cock-roaches. Doors of popular tea-rooms were pulled apart and from them there burst a soapy cloud, as from a laundry. Strange, as though it had become warmer in the street, as though it had turned into spring, when men ran cheer-ing, with bent backs, down the street and their felt shoes and primitive stockings flashed as they ran. The pigeons were not afraid of the crowd. They flew along the road in search of food. Milletseed, oats and dung-seed were spread on the pavement in the snow. A cake-stall shone with grease and warmth. And this heat and polish fell into mouths rinsed with corn-brandy. The grease inflamed their throats. Afterwards it escaped by way of their palpitating chests. Perhaps it was this that warmed the street.

And then suddenly it became empty. Twilight fell. The peasant sleighs drove without passengers, low sleighs moved swiftly, loaded with long-bearded men sunk in their fur coats, running amok, throwing them over their backs, clasping them with the caresses of a bear. From them there fell tufts of dull-coloured hay on the street and the slow, sweet thaw of distant sleigh-bells. The merchants vanished at the end of the road, beyond the grove of small birch trees, which from there resembled palings torn apart.

Hither came the crows who, croaking expansively, flew above the home of the Luvers. Only here they did not croak. Here, shouting and flapping their wings, they scur-ried to the fence-wall and then suddenly, as though at a given signal, threw themselves at the trees and hustling and elbowing, took their places on the bare branches. One felt then how late—how late—it was in all the world. So late indeed that it could be expressed by no clock.

. . . . .

So a week passed, and at the second week, on Thursday

at dawn, she again saw him. Lisa's bed was empty. When she woke up, Zhenia heard the wicket-gate as it banged behind her. She got up and without lighting a light went to the little window. It was still dark. She felt that the sky, the branches of the trees and the dog's romping were as oppressive as on the previous day. The overclouded weather had lasted for three days, which were without the strength to remove it from the friable street, like a cast-iron cauldron from a ragged floorboard.

The lamp burnt in the window across the road. Two bars of light fell on a horse and lay on its tufted pasterns. Shadows moved on the snow, the arms of a ghost wrapped in a fur coat moved, the light moved in a curtained window. The horse stood motionless, dreaming.

Then she saw him. Immediately she recognised him by his silhouette. The lame man lifted his lamp and began to move away with it. Behind him moved the two brilliant bars of white light, which contracted and expanded, and after the bars moved the sleighs which quickly flashed by and even more quickly plunged into darkness, as they moved slowly behind the house towards the porch.

It was strange that Tsvetkov should continue to come into her field of vision, here in the suburbs. But Zhenia was not amazed. It made little impression upon her. Soon the lamp reappeared, moving smoothly, smoothly across all the curtains: it began to move back again, until suddenly it paused behind the curtain on the window-sill from where it had been removed.

It was on the Thursday. On the Friday they came for her.

IX

Ten days after she had returned home, after more than three weeks' holiday had interrupted the customary course of her life, Zhenia learned the rest from her teacher. After lunch the doctor packed his things and went away. And she asked him to pay her respects to the house in which he had examined her in the spring, and all the streets and Kama river. He expressed the hope that it would no longer be necessary to summon him from Perm. She went with him to the gate—the man who had made her tremble so much on the first morning after her journey from the Deffendovs—while her mother slept and they refused to let her see her, and when she asked what illness her mother was suffering from he began by reminding her of the night when her parents went to the theatre. And how at the end of the play, they went out and the stallion . . .

"Vikormish?"

"Yes, if that's his name. Well then, Vikormish began to stamp and trample underfoot, and he trampled down a man who chanced to be passing by."

"Trampled to death?"

"Unfortunately, yes."

"But mother . . ."

"But mother . . ."

"Your mother suffered a nervous breakdown . . ." He smiled, barely able to adapt for the girl his own Latin "partus praematurus."

"And then my dead brother was born?"

"Who told you? Yes."

"And then, in front of them all? Or did they find it already dead? Don't tell me! Oh, how terrible! Now I understand. He was already dead, otherwise I would have heard him. You see, I was reading. Late at night. So I would have heard. But when did he live? Doctor, do such things happen? I even went into the bedroom. He was dead. He must have been dead."

How lucky it was that she had seen the man from the Deffendovs the day before at dawn; while the accident at the theatre took place three weeks ago. How happy she was to have recognised him. Confusedly she thought that if

227

she had not seen him all this time, she would now, after hearing the doctor's words, believe that it was the lame man who had been trampled underfoot at the theatre.

And now, after staying with them all that time and becoming one of them, the doctor was going. In the evening her tutor arrived. It was washing day. In the kitchen they were putting the laundry through the mangle. The hoarfrost left the window-pane and the garden came closer to the window, and becoming entangled in the lace curtains approached the table. Into the conversation came short, rumbling sounds from the mangle. Dikikh, like everyone else, found that she had changed. And she noticed the change in him.

"Why are you so sad?"

"Am I? It is quite possible. I have lost a friend."

"So you are sad too? So many deaths—and everything so suddenly—" she sighed.

But he had no time to say what he knew, before something inexplicable occurred. Suddenly the girl followed other thoughts about the number of deaths, obviously forgetting the calmer arguments which could be adduced from the lamp she had seen that morning, she said anxiously, "Wait a moment. You went to the tobacconist the day Negarat was leaving. I saw you with someone. Was it him?" She was afraid to say Tsvetkov.

Dikikh became silent as he heard the intonation of these words; he searched in his memory until at last he remembered that they really went there for some paper and to ask for a complete set of Turgeniev for Madame Luvers; and in fact he was there while the dead man was there. She shuddered, and tears sprang from her eyes. But the important thing was still to come.

When, after telling her with prolonged silences in which they heard the squeal of the mangle, what sort of youth he had been and from what a good family he was descended, Dikikh lit his cigarette and Zhenia remembered with horror that this was the interval which separated her tutor from the repetitions of the doctor's story, and when he made an attempt to utter a few words, among which was the word 'theatre,' Zhenia screamed in a voice which was not her own and threw herself out of the room.

Dikikh listened. Except for the sound of the mangle, there was no other sound in the house. He stood up, exactly like a stork. He pulled a long face and raised one leg, ready to go to her help. He hurried in search of the girl, deciding that there was no one at home and that she had fainted. And while he was knocking in the dark against riddles of wood, wool and metal, the girl sat in a corner and cried. He continued his search, but in his thoughts he was already lifting her half-dead from the carpet. He shuddered when, behind his elbows a loud voice cried out in tears. "I'm here. Look out for the cupboard. Wait for me in the classroom. I'll be there immediately."

The curtains fell to the floor and the starlit winter light beyond the window reached the floor, and below, waist-deep in the snowdrifts, trailing the glittering flails of their branches in the deep snow, the thick trees rambled towards the clear light of the window. And somewhere beyond the wall, tightly drawn together by the sheets, backwards and forwards came the heavy groans of the mangle. "How can we explain this tremendous sensitivity?" the tutor muttered. "Obviously the dead man stood in an important relation to the girl. She has completely changed." He had explained recurring decimals to a child but the girl who had just this minute sent him into the classroom . . . and this was the affair of a month? Obviously the dead man had somehow produced a deep and indelible impression upon her. There was a name for this kind of sentiment. How strange! He gave her lessons every other day and understood nothing. She was so very sympathetic, and he was

229

desperately sorry for her. But when will she cry her eyes out and come out of it all? Probably all the others were away. He was sorry for her from the bottom of his soul. A remarkable night.

He was mistaken. The sentiment he imagined played no part in the affair. But he was not entirely mistaken. The sentiments which lay concealed in all this were ineffaceable. They went deeper than he supposed . . . They lay outside the girl's control because they were deeply alive and significant, and their significance lay in the fact that it was the first time *another man* entered her life, a third person, entirely indifferent to her, without a name or even a fortuitous name, inspiring neither hatred nor love, but *the one whom the commandments bore in mind when* they said: Thou shalt not murder, thou shalt not steal, and other things. They said: "*You who are individual and alive must not commit against the confused and universal that which you do not want it to do to you.*" Dikikh was mistaken when he thought there was a name for sentiments of this kind. There is no name.

Zhenia cried because she considered herself guilty in everything. It was she who had introduced him into the life of the family on the day when she saw him behind the strange garden, and saw him unnecessarily, purposelessly, thoughtlessly, and she began to meet him afterwards at every step, directly and obliquely, and even, as it happened on the last occasion, against all probability.

When she saw the book Dikikh was taking from the shelf, she knit her brows and said, "No. I don't want to do lessons from it to-day. Put the book back in its place. I'm sorry. Forgive me."

And without further words Lermontov was squeezed by the same hand into a disorderly row of classics.

(1918)   *Translated by Robert Payne*

SELECTED POEMS

Translated by C. M. Bowra

Sparrow Hills

Kisses on the breast, like water from a pitcher!
Not always, not ceaseless spurts the summer's well.
Nor shall we raise up the hurdy-gurdy's clamour
Each night from the dust with feet that stamp and trail.

I have heard of age,—those hideous forebodings!
When no wave will lift its hands up to the stars.
If they speak, you doubt it. No face in the meadows,
No heart in the pools, and no god in the firs.

Rouse your soul to frenzy. Let to-day come foaming.
It's the world's midday. Have you no eyes for it?
Look how in the heights thoughts seethe into white
    bubbles
Of fir-cones, woodpeckers, clouds, pine-needles, heat.

Here the rails are ended of the city tram-cars.
Further, pines must do. Further, trams cannot pass.
Further, it is Sunday. Plucking down the branches,
Skipping through the clearings, slipping on the grass.

Sifting midday light and Whitsunday and walking
Wodds would have us think the world is always so;
They're so planned with thickets, so inspired with spaces,
Fallen from the clouds on us, like chintz below.

Summer

Athirst for insects, butterflies,
And stains we long had waited,
And round us both were memories
Of heat, mint, honey plaited.

No clocks chimed, but the flail rang clear
From dawn to dusk and planted
Its dreams of stings into the air,
The weather was enchanted.

Strolled sunset to its heart's content,
They yielded to cicadas
And stars and trees its government
Of gardens and of larders.

The moon in absence, out of sight,
Not shade but baulks was throwing,
And softly, softly the shy night
From cloud to cloud was flowing.

From dream more than from roof, and more
Forgetful than faint-hearted,
Soft rain was shuffling at the door
And smell of wine-corks spurted.

So smelt the dust. So smelt the grass
And if we chanced to heed them,
Smell from the gentry's teaching was
Of brotherhood and freedom.

The councils met in villages;
Weren't you with those that held them?
Bright with wood-sorrel hung the days,
And smell of wine-corks filled them.

In the Wood

A lilac heat was heavy on the meadow,
High in the wood cathedral's darkness swelled.
What in the world was left still for their kisses?
It was all theirs, soft wax in fingers held.

Such is the dream—you do not sleep, but only
Dream that you thirst for sleep, that someone lies
Asleep, and through his dream beneath his eyelids
Two black suns sear the lashes of his eyes.

Rays flowed, and with the ebbing flowed the beetles:
Upon his cheeks the dragon-flies' gloss stirs.
The wood was full of careful scintillations
As under pincers at the clockmaker's.

It seemed he slumbered to the tick of figures,
While in harsh amber high above they set
Their nicely tested clocks up in the ether
And regulate and move them to the heat.

They shift them round about, and shake the needles,
Scatter shadow, and swing, and bore a place
For darkness like a mast erected upward
In day's decline upon its blue clock-face.

It seems that ancient happiness flits over;
It seems sleep's setting holds the woodland close.
Those who are happy do not watch clocks ticking,
But sleep, it seems, is all this couple does.

Poem

The air is whipped by the frequent rain-drops;
The ice is grey and mangy. Ahead
You look for the skyline to awaken
And start; you wait for the drone to spread.

As always, with overcoat unbuttoned,
With muffler about his chest undone,
He pursues before him the unsleeping
Silly birds and chases them on.

Now he comes to see you and, dishevelled,
The dripping candles he tries to snuff,
Yawns and remembers that now's the moment
To take the hyacinth's night-cap off.

Out of his senses, ruffling his hair-mop,
Dark in his thoughts' confusion, he
Leaves you quite dumbfounded with a wicked
Stupid tale that he tells of me.

Spasskoye

Unforgettable September is strewn about Spasskoye,
Is to-day not time to leave the cottage here?
Beyond the fence Echo has shouted with the herdsman,
And in the woods has made the axe's stroke ring clear.

Last night outside the park the chilling marshes shivered.
The moment the sun rose it disappeared again.
The hare-bells will not drink of the rheumatic dew-drops,
On birches dropsy swells a dirty lilac stain.

The wood is melancholy. What it needs is quiet
Under the snows in bear-dens' unawaking sleep.
And there among the boles inside the blackened fences
Jaws of the columned park, like a long death-list, gape.

The birchwood has not ceased to blot and lose its colour,
To thin its watery shadows and grow sparse and dim.
He is still mumbling,—you're fifteen years old again now,
And now again, my child, what shall we do with them?

So many of them now that you should give up playing.
They're like birds in bushes, mushrooms along hedges.
Now with them we've begun to curtain our horizon
And with their mist to hide another's distances.

On his death-night the clown hears tumult, typhus-stricken
The gods' Homeric laughter from the gallery.
Now from the road, in Spasskoye, on the timbered cottage
Looks in hallucination the same agony.

Poem

Stars raced headlong. Seaward headlands lathered.
Salt spray blinded. Eyes dried up their tears.
Darkness filled the bedrooms. Thoughts raced headlong.
To Sahara Sphinx turned patient ears.

Candles guttered. Blood, it seemed, was frozen
In the huge Colossus. Lips at play
Swelled into the blue smile of the desert.
In that hour of ebb night sank away.

Seas were stirred by breezes from Morocco.
Simoon blew. Archangel snored in snows.
Candles guttered. First text of The Prophet
Dried, and on the Ganges dawn arose.

January 1919

That year! How often "Out you fall!"
That old year's whisper at my window said.
The new year makes an end of all
And brings a Dickens Christmas tale instead.

He murmurs: "Shake yourself, forget."
Mercury rises with the sun outside,
Just as the old year strychnine set
And fell down in the glass from cyanide.

For by his hand and by his dawn
And by his hair that indolently stirs
Outside the window Peace is drawn
From birds and roofs as from philosophers.

Now here he comes, lies in the light
That shines from panels and from snow out there.
He's boisterous and impolite,
Shouts, calls for drink,—it is too much to bear.

He's off his head. With him he brings
The hubbub of the yard. What can you do?
In all the world no sufferings
Are such that they will not be cured by snow.

May It Be

Dawn shakes the candle, shoots a flame
To light the wren and does not miss.
I search my memories and proclaim:
"May life be always fresh as this!"

Like a shot dawn rang through the night,
Bang-bang it went. In swooning flight

The wads of bullets flame and hiss.
May life be always fresh as this.

The breeze is at the door again.
At night he shivered, wanted us.
He froze when daybreak came with rain.
May life be always fresh as this.

He is astonishingly queer.
Why rudely past the gateman press?
Of course he saw "No entrance here."
May life be always fresh as this.

Still with a handkerchief to shake,
While mistress still, chase all about,—
While yet our darkness does not break,
While yet the flames have not gone out.

Poem

So they begin. With two years gone
From nurse to countless tunes they scuttle.
They chirp and whistle. Then comes on
The third year, and they start to prattle.

So they begin to see and know.
In din of started turbines roaring
Mother seems not their mother now,
And you not you, and home is foreign.

What meaning has the menacing
Beauty beneath the lilac seated,
If to steal children's not the thing?
So first they fear that they are cheated.

So ripen fears. Can he endure
A start to bear him in successes,
When he's a Faust, a sorcerer?
So first his gipsy life progresses.

So from the fence where home should lie
In flight above are found to hover
Seas unexpected as a sigh.
So first iambics they discover.

So summer nights fall down and pray
"Thy will be done" where oats are sprouting,
And menace with your eyes the day.
So with the sun they start disputing.

So verses start them on their way.

Poem

Love is for some a heavy cross,
But in you there is no contortion,
The key to life's enigma is
The charm that is your secret portion.

In spring rustling is heard again,
And news and truths that ripple running.
Your race has sprung from such a strain;
Like air, your mind is free from cunning.

Easy to wake, again to see,
To shake out the heart's wordy litter,
Nor henceforth choked in life to be,—
No need for skill in such a matter.

Poem

If I had known what would come later,
When first my stage career began,
The words will take to blood and slaughter,
Go for the throat and kill a man,

To play with such a tangled living,
Point-blank refusal I'd have made,—
So far away was my beginning
My first concern was so afraid.

But age is Rome, which in impatience
Of quips and somersaults, would cry
Not for an actor's recitations
But that in earnest he should die.

Feelings dictate a line and send it,
A slave upon the stage, and that
Means that the task of art is ended,
And there's a breath of earth and fate.

Summer Day

In spring before the dawn we see
Heaps in the kitchen garden,
As pagans for fertility
Their festal altars burden.

The fresh-cut clods flame in my plot;
In steams at early morning,
And all the earth becomes red-hot
Just like an oven burning.

239

I cast aside this shirt of mine
Where my earth-labour takes me;
The heat strikes down upon my spine
And like wet clay it bakes me.

I stand up where the sun's rays beat;
With screwed-up eyes I burnish
Myself from head to foot with heat,
As with a fiery varnish.

Night, bursting on the corridor
Comes to my sleeping quarter
And leaves me brimming like a jar
With lilac and with water.

The upper layer she wipes away
From cooling walls, and laden
With me for gift she offers me
To any country maiden.

Spring 1944

This spring there is a change in everything.
More lively is the sparrows' riot.
I shall not even try to tell of it,
How bright my soul is and how quiet.

My thoughts and writings are quite different,
And from the choir's loud octaves singing
The mighty voice of earth is audible
Of liberated countries ringing.

The breath of spring across this land of ours
Wipes winter's marks from off its spaces

And washes off black rings that tears have made
Round red eyes of Slavonic faces.

The grass is waiting everywhere to burst,
And though in ancient Prague the alleys
Are silent, each more crooked than the rest,
They'll burst in song soon, like the gullies.

From Czech, Moravian and Serbian,
By the soft hands of spring uplifted;
Tales tear away the sheet of lawlessness
And burst with buds where snow has drifted.

All will be dim in the mist of fairy-tales,
Like patterns on the wall that dazzle
In golden chambers where the Boyars lived
Or on the great church of St. Basil.

A dreamer and a thinker in the night,
Moscow is dearer than the world. Her dower
Is to be home and source of everything
With which the centuries will flower.

Translated by Babette Deutsch

"The Drowsy Garden"

The drowsy garden scatters insects
Bronze as the ash from braziers blown.
Level with me and with my candle,
Hang flowering worlds, their leaves full grown.

As into some unheard-of dogma
I move across into this night,
Where a worn poplar age has grizzled
Screens the moon's strip of fallow light,

Where the pond lies, an open secret,
Where apple bloom is surf and sigh,
And where the garden, a lake dwelling,
Holds out in front of it the sky.

The Urals for the First Time

Without an accoucheuse, in darkness, pushing her
Blind hands against the night, the Ural fastness, torn and
Half-dead with agony, was screaming in a blur
Of mindless pain, as she was giving birth to morning.

And brushed by chance, tall ranges far and wide
Loosed toppling bronze pell-mell in thunder-colored rum-
    bling.
The train panted and coughed, clutching the mountain-
    side,
And at that sound the ghosts of fir trees shied and
    stumbled.

The smoky dawn was a narcotic for the peaks,
A drug with which the fire-breathing dragon plied them,
As when a specious thief upon a journey seeks
To lull his fellow travelers with opium slipped them slyly.

They woke on fire. The skies were poppy-colored flame,
Whence Asiatics skied like hunters after quarry;
To kiss the forests' feet the eager strangers came
And thrust upon the firs the regal crowns they carried.

Arrayed in majesty, by rank the firs arose,
Those shaggy dynasts, their grave glory clamant,
And trod the orange velvet of the frozen snows
Spread on a tinseled cloth and richly damasked.

Spring

How many buds, how many sticky butts
Of candles, April kindled, now are glued
Fast to the boughs! The park is redolent
Of puberty. The woods' retorts are rude.

The forest's throat is caught in a thick knot
Of feathered throats: a lassoed buffalo
Bellowing in the nets as organs pant:
Wrestlers who groan sonatas, deep and slow.

Oh, poetry, be a Greek sponge supplied
With suction pads, a thing that soaks and cleaves,
For I would lay you on the wet green bench
Out in the garden, among sticky leaves.

Grow sumptuous frills, fabulous hoopskirts, swell,
And suck in clouds, roulades, ravines, until
Night comes; then, poetry, I'll squeeze you out
And let the thirsty paper drink its fill.

Three Variations

1

When consummate the day hangs before you,
Each detail to be scanned at your ease,
Just the sultry chatter of squirrels
Resounds in the resinous trees.

And storing up strength in their languor,
The ranked piney heights are adrowse.
While the freckled sweat is pouring
From the peeling forest's boughs.

243

2

Miles thick with torpor nauseate the gardens.
The catalepsy of the valleys' rage
Is weightier, more threatening than a tempest,
Fiercer than hurricane's most savage raid.

The storm is near. The dry mouth of the garden
Gives off the smell of nettles, roofs, and fear,
And of corruption; and the cattle's bellow
Rises columnar in the static air.

3

Now tatters of denuded clouds
Grow on each bush in tasseled groves.
Damp nettles fill the garden's mouth.
It smells of storms and treasure troves.

The shrubs are tired of lament.
In heaven arched prospects multiply.
Like web-toed birds on swampy ground
The barefoot azure treads the sky.

And willow branches and the leaves
Of oaks, and tracks beside the spring,
Like lips the hand has not wiped dry,
Are glistening, are glistening.

Improvisation

A flock of keys I had feeding out of my hand,
To clapping of wings and croaking and feathery fight;
On tiptoe I stood and stretched out my arm, and the sleeve
Rolled up, so I felt at my elbow the nudging of night.

And the dark. And a pond in the dark, and the lapping of
    waves.
And the birds of the species I-love-you that others deny
Would be killed, so it seemed, before the savage black
    beaks,
The strong and the strident, were ever to falter and die.

And a pond. And the dark. And festive the palpitant flares
From pipkins of midnight pitch. And the boat's keel
    gnawed
By the wave. And always the greedy noise of the birds
Who fighting over the elbow fluttered and cawed.

The gullets of dams were agurgle, gulping the night.
And the mother birds, if the fledglings on whom they
    dote
Were not to be fed, would kill, so it seemed, before
The roulades would die in the strident, the crooked throat.

Out of Superstition

The cubbyhole I live in is a box
    Of candied orange peel.
Soiled by hotel rooms till I reach the morgue—
    That's not for me, I feel.

Out of pure superstition I have come
    And settled here once more.
The wallpaper is brown as any oak,
    And there's a singing door.

I kept one hand upon the latch, you tried
    To fight free of the nets,
And forelock touched enchanted forelock, and
    Then lips touched violets.

O softy, in the name of times long gone,
  You play the old encore:
Your costume like a primrose chirps "Hello"
  To April as before.

It's wrong to think—you are no vestal: you
  Brought in a chair one day,
Stood on it, took my life down from the shelf
  And blew the dust away.

"Waving a Bough"

Waving a bough full of fragrance,
In the dark, with pure good to sup,
The water the storm had made giddy
Went running from cup to cup.

From chalice to chalice rolling,
It slid along two and hung,
One drop of agate, within them,
Shining and shy it clung.

Over the meadowsweet blowing,
The wind may torture and tear
At that drop—it will never divide it,
Nor the kissing, the drinking pair.

They laugh and try to shake free and
Stand up, each straight as a dart,
But the drop will not leave the stigmas,
Wild horses won't tear them apart.

"Fresh Paint"

I should have seen the sign: "Fresh paint,"
  But useless to advise
The careless soul, and memory's stained
  With cheeks, calves, hands, lips, eyes.

More than all failure, all success,
  I loved you, for your skill
In whitening the yellowed world
  As white cosmetics will.

Listen, my dark, my friend: by God,
  All will grow white somehow,
Whiter than madness or lamp shades
  Or bandage on a brow.

Definition of the Soul

To fly off, a ripe pear in a storm,
With one leaf clinging on as it must.
Mad devotion! It quitted the branch!
It will choke with its throat full of dust!

A ripe pear, more aslant than the wind.
What devotion! "You'll bray me? You're brash!"
Look! In beauty the thunder-spent storm
Has blazed out, crumbled down—sunk to ash.

And our birthplace is burned to a crisp.
Say, fledgling, where now is your nest?
O my leaf, with the fears of a finch!
My shy silk, why still fight and protest?

247

Rest in concrement, song, unafraid.
Whither now? All striving is naught.
Ah, "here": mortal adverb! The throb
Of concrescence could give it no thought.

Rupture

The piano, aquiver, will lick the foam from its lips.
The frenzy will wrench you, fell you, and you, undone,
Will whisper: "Darling!" "No," I shall cry, "what's this?
In the presence of music!" Of nearness there is none

Like twilight's, with the chords tossed into the fireplace
Like fluttering diaries, for one year, and two, and three.
O miraculous obit, beckon, beckon! You may
Well be astonished. For—look—you are free.

I do not hold you. Go, yes, go elsewhere,
Do good. *Werther* cannot be written again,
And in our time death's odor is in the air:
To open a window is to open a vein.

1918

"Here the Trace"

Here the trace of enigma's strange fingernail shows.
"It is late. Let me sleep, and at dawn I'll reread
And then all will be clear. Till they wake me, there's none
Who can move the beloved as I move her, indeed!"

How I moved you! You bent to the brass of my lips
As an audience stirred by a tragedy thrills.
Ah, that kiss was like summer. It lingered, delayed,
Swelling slow to a storm as it topples and spills.

As the birds drink, I drank. Till I swooned still I sucked.
As they flow through the gullet, the stars seem to stop.
But the nightingales shuddering roll their bright eyes,
As they drain the vast vault of the night, drop by drop.

1918

Spring

I've come from the street, Spring, where the poplar stands
Amazed, where distance quails, and the house fears it will
    fall,
Where the air is blue, like the bundle of wash in the hands
Of the convalescent leaving the hospital;

Where evening is empty: a tale begun by a star
And interrupted, to the confusion of rank
On rank of clamorous eyes, waiting for what they are
Never to know, their bottomless gaze blank.

1918

"We're Few"

We're few, perhaps three, hellish fellows
Who hail from the flaming Donetz,
With a fluid gray bark for our cover
Made of rain clouds and soldiers' soviets
And verses and endless debates
About art or it may be freight rates.

We used to be people. We're epochs.
Pell-mell we rush caravanwise
As the tundra to groans of the tender
And tension of pistons and ties.
Together we'll rip through your prose,
We'll whirl, a tornado of crows,

And be off! But you'll not understand it
Till late. So the wind in the dawn
Hits the thatch on the roof—for a moment—
But puts immortality on
At trees' stormy sessions, in speech
Of boughs the roof's shingles can't reach.

1921

"You Pictures Flying"

You pictures flying slantwise in a shower
From the highway that blew the candle out,
I can't teach you to keep from rhyme and measure,
Deserting hooks and walls in your skew rout.

Suppose the universe goes masked? Or even
That every latitude breeds some of those
Who are on hand to stop its mouth with putty
And seal it for the winter: just suppose!

Yet objects tear their masks off, all their power
Leaks out, they leave their honor where it lies,
Should there be any reason for their singing,
Should the occasion for a shower arise.

1922

Roosters

Nightlong the water labored breathlessly.
Till morning came, the rain burned linseed oil.
Now vapor from beneath the lilac lid
Pours forth: earth steams like *shchee* that's near the boil.

And when the grass, shaking itself, leaps up,
Oh, who will tell the dew how scared I am—
The moment the first cock begins to yawp,
And then one more, and then—the lot of them?

They name the years as these roll by in turn,
And on each darkness, as it goes, they call,
Foretelling thus the change that is to come
To rain, to earth, to love—to each and all.

1923

To a Friend

Come, don't I know that, stumbling against shadows,
Darkness could never have arrived at light?
Do I rate happy hundreds over millions
Of happy men? Am I a monster quite?

Isn't the Five-Year Plan a yardstick for me,
Its rise and fall my own? But I don't quiz
In asking: What shall I do with my thorax
And with what's slower than inertia is?

The great Soviet gives to the highest passions
In these brave days each one its rightful place,
Yet vainly leaves one vacant for the poet.
When that's not empty, look for danger's face.

Lyubka

Not long ago the rain walked through this clearing
Like a surveyor. Now with tinsel bait
The lily of the valley's leaves are weighted,
And water got into the mullein's ears.

These are the frigid fir trees' quondam nurslings,
Their ear lobes stretched with dew; they shun the day,
And grow apart, single and solitary,
Even their odors separately disbursed.

When it is teatime in the summer villas,
The fog fills the mosquito's sail, and night,
Plucking the strings of a guitar but lightly,
Stands among pansies in a mistlike milk.

Then with nocturnal violet all is scented.
Faces and years. And thoughts. And every event
That from the thievish past can be commanded
And in the future taken from Fate's hand.

1927

"We Were in Georgia"

From "Waves"

We were in Georgia. You can get this land
If hell is multiplied by paradise,
Bare indigence by tenderness, and if
A hothouse serves as pedestal for ice.

And then you'll know what subtle doses of
Success and labor, duty, mountain air
Make the right mixture with the earth and sky
For man to be the way we found him there.

So that he grew, in famine and defeat
And bondage, to this stature, without fault,
Becoming thus a model and a mold,
Something as stable and as plain as salt.

1931

"The Caucasus"

The Caucasus lay spread before our gaze,
An unmade bed, it seemed, with tousled sheets;
The blue ice of the peaks more fathomless
Than the warmed chasms with their harbored heats.

Massed in the mist and out of sorts, it reared
The steady malice of its icy crests
As regularly as the salvoes spat
In an engagement from machine-gun nests.

And staring at this beauty with the eyes
Of the brigades whose task it was to seize
The region, how I envied those who had
Palpable obstacles to face like these.

O if we had their luck! If, out of time,
As though it peered through fog, this day of ours,
Our program, were of such substantial stuff,
And frowned down at us as this rough steep lours!

Then day and night our program would march on,
Setting its heel upon my prophecies,
Kneading their downpour with the very sole
Of its straight backbone into verities.

There would be no one I could quarrel with,
And not another hour would I give
To making verses: unbeknown to all,
No poet's life, but poems I would live.

1931

"If Only, When I Made My Début"

If only, when I made my début,
There might have been a way to tell
That lines with blood in them can murder,
That they can flood the throat and kill,

I certainly would have rejected
A jest on such a sour note,
So bashful was that early interest,
The start was something so remote.

But age is pagan Rome, demanding
No balderdash, no measured breath,
No fine feigned parody of dying,
But really being done to death.

A line that feeling sternly dictates
Sends on the stage a slave, and, faith,
It is good-bye to art forever
Then, then things smack of soil and Fate.

New Directions Paperbooks—A Partial Listing

For complete listing request free catalog from
New Directions, 80 Eighth Avenue, New York 10011

†Bilingual